Mathematical Knowledge
of
Japanese, Chinese, and American
Elementary School Children

James W. Stigler
University of Chicago

Shin-Ying Lee and Harold W. Stevenson
University of Michigan

NATIONAL COUNCIL OF TEACHERS OF
MATHEMATICS

Library of Congress Cataloging-in-Publication Data

Stigler, James W.
 Mathematical knowledge of Japanese, Chinese, and American
elementary school children / James W. Stigler, Shin-Ying Lee, and
Harold W. Stevenson.
  p. cm.
 Includes bibliographical references.
 ISBN 0-87353-294-5
 1. Mathematics—Study and teaching (Elementary). 2. Mathematical
ability—Testing. I. Lee, Shin-Ying. II. Stevenson, Harold W.
(Harold William), 1924-   III. Title.
QA135.5.S75 1990
372.7—dc20   90-36064
                                                                  CIP

Printed in the United States of America

CONTENTS

ACKNOWLEDGMENTS

The research reported here was funded by grants BNS8409372 and MDR8751390 from the National Science Foundation. Writing was completed while the first author was a Fellow at the Center for Advanced Study in the Behavioral Sciences, supported in part by a grant from the Spencer Foundation, and a Fellow of the John Simon Guggenheim Memorial Foundation. We would like to thank the numerous colleagues who participated in this study: our collaborators in Japan were Professors Seiro Kitamura and Susumu Kimura at Tohoku Fukushi College in Sendai; and in Taiwan, Professor Lian-wen Mao of Taipei Municipal Teachers College. We are grateful to Sheila Sconiers for her assistance in constructing the mathematics tests; to Michelle Perry for coordinating data collection in Chicago; and to all the teachers, parents, and children who participated in this study.

INTRODUCTION

INTEREST in the comparative study of the mathematical abilities of American and Asian students has increased greatly in recent years. The reason is clear. Asian students consistently outperform their American counterparts in tests of mathematics achievement. The poor performance of the American students compels us to try to understand the reasons for this difference in performance. Without a knowledge of mathematics, our nation's ability to advance in science and technology is severely limited.

The fact that Japanese middle and high school students outscore American students on tests of mathematics achievement has been known for at least twenty years, since the publication of the first International Association for the Evaluation of Education (IEA) study. This study measured achievement in several mathematical topics among eighth and twelfth graders in twelve countries (Husén 1967). The second IEA study (McKnight et al. 1987) compared eighth graders in twenty countries and twelfth graders in fifteen countries. Both studies measured the abilities of (1) eighth-grade students to solve problems in arithmetic, algebra, geometry, statistics, and measurement, and (2) twelfth-grade students to solve problems in algebra, geometry, elementary functions and calculus, probability and statistics, sets and relations, and number theory.

The most salient results to emerge from both studies have been the outstanding performance of Japanese students and the mediocre performance of American students. However, despite the alarm such results have generated among policymakers and to some degree among the general public, it is not easy to use this information to begin to remedy the difficult situation that faces the United States. The results tell us nothing about when in children's development the cross-national differences in mathematics achievement begin to emerge. Also, by the time students have reached middle school, there are important curricular differences between countries—including the number and content of mathematics courses taken, the materials used, and the goals of the curriculum—as well as differences in the percentage of children attending school. These differences make it difficult to evaluate the meaning of the cross-national findings. If the differences arise only during the middle school years when the content of mathematics becomes increasingly abstract and complex, then the situation suggests reform and remediation. If, however, the differences are evident at the elementary school level, then a path of prevention would be indicated.

1

This particular issue has been addressed in reports from our previous study of achievement differences between elementary school children in Japan, Taiwan, and the United States (Stevenson, Lee, and Stigler 1986; Stigler et al. 1982). In that study—conducted with large samples of first- and fifth-grade children in Sendai (Japan), Taipei (Taiwan), and the Minneapolis metropolitan area—we found highly significant differences between the scores obtained by Chinese and Japanese first graders and those of their American counterparts. Differences were even greater at fifth grade. For example, in comparing the average scores on the tests of the mathematics achievement of twenty fifth-grade classrooms in each of the three locations, we found that the highest-scoring American classroom obtained an average score lower than that of the lowest-scoring Japanese classroom and of all but one of the twenty classrooms in Taipei (Stevenson, Lee, and Stigler 1986). This increasing divergence of Asian and American performance through the elementary school years has been replicated in a study of Korean and American children (Song and Ginsburg 1987). Although similar results from studies of high school students could be partially due to selective attendance at school or to enrollment in advanced mathematics courses, such explanations cannot apply to studies of elementary school students. In Japan and Taiwan, as in the United States, attendance at school is required through the elementary school years.

The test we used to evaluate mathematics achievement was based on a detailed analysis of the mathematics curricula in the three locations and was judged culturally fair by our colleagues and professionals in the three locations. Although the test included both computation and word problems, there may have been an overemphasis on computational skills and insufficient emphasis on the creative problem-solving skills that American mathematics educators consider to be of great importance. Nevertheless, American children received lower scores on both computational and problem-solving items in the test. Before concluding that American elementary school children demonstrate a broad range of deficiencies in mathematics, however, we need more detailed descriptions of the aspects of mathematics in which Asian and American children differ. Without such detailed information, it is difficult to know which aspects of mathematics require greater attention in American classrooms.

We designed the present study partially to respond to these points and to evaluate as many aspects of elementary school mathematics as possible. After reviewing the mathematics textbooks used in each location and discussing our goal with mathematics educators, we constructed a battery of tests of the core elementary school mathematics curriculum. We constructed two types of tests: group tests of computational skills and tests of knowledge and skill in mathematics administered to one child at a time. The individual tests included word problems, conceptual knowledge, mathematical operations, graphing, estimation, visualization, transformation of spatial relations, and mental calculation.

Overview of the Study

As in our earlier study, we selected Sendai, Japan, and Taipei, Taiwan. However, we chose Chicago rather than Minneapolis as our United States site primarily because we believe that Chicago is a more representative American city. First- and fifth-grade children were tested in three sessions. In the first session, all children in each classroom visited were given the group test of computation. Fifth graders were also given a group test of geometry. The second and third sessions required a total of two hours of one-to-one testing for each child. The battery of nine tests was administered in these two sessions. The first session was conducted at the equivalent time in the school year in all three locations—during the fall of 1985 in Taipei and Chicago, where the school year begins in September, and in the spring of 1986 in Sendai, where the school year begins in April. The second and third sessions were held approximately five months after the first session.

The data are presented in two main parts. In the first part, we will discuss the results of the group testing of computation. The second part contains a report of the results of the individually administered tests.

We have presented the results in detail in order to give the fullest picture of the strengths and weaknesses in the children's knowledge of mathematics. All items in each test, along with the percentages of students in each city responding correctly to each item, are presented in the appendixes. The results of the group tests appear in Appendix A and the individual tests in Appendix B.

GROUP TESTING OF COMPUTATIONAL SKILLS

Mathematical knowledge, even at the elementary school level, is a fuzzy concept. At the edges of the concept, there is controversy over what exactly should be considered mathematical, and particularly over what should constitute the aims of elementary mathematics education. Some of these boundary topics, like estimation and visualization skills, are seldom assessed in standardized tests of mathematics achievement. However, there is little disagreement about what is prototypical of elementary mathematics. Computational skills form a major part of what is taught to elementary school children. Because computational skills are easily assessed, we decided to use group testing in evaluating computational skills. We were able to test large samples of children and sample a broad range of each child's computational skills.

Method

Description of the test. The first-grade computation test consisted of forty-one items; the fifth-grade test, fifty items. All tests in the study were constructed after an intensive analysis of the content of the mathematics textbooks used in each location. The detailed information obtained from our analysis made it possible to determine for each item whether students in each city had been exposed to the information necessary to solve the item. The items were arranged in order of difficulty from the kindergarten level through the sixth-grade level. Members of each culture participated in the construction of the test, and after preliminary versions were constructed, the tests were sent to our colleagues in Japan and Taiwan for their criticism and suggestions. We are confident, therefore, that the tests are appropriate for the grade levels being tested and are culturally fair for children in each of these three cultures.

Selection of the sample. The study was conducted in elementary schools in Sendai, Japan; Taipei, Taiwan; and the Chicago metropolitan area (i.e., Cook County) of the United States. In both Sendai and Taipei, ten schools in each city were selected to represent the geographic and socioeconomic diversity of these cities. The population of Chicago, though, is more diverse racially, ethnically, linguistically, and socioeconomically than the population of either of the two Asian cities. Therefore we decided to sample twenty schools to represent the Chicago area. Our final sample was selected in conjunction with researchers at the Chicago Board of Education and with demographers familiar with the Chicago metropolitan area. We included in our Chicago sample schools that are predominantly white, black, Hispanic, and ethnically mixed; schools that draw from upper, middle, and lower socioeconomic groups; schools that are public and private; and schools that are urban and suburban. The diversity of the schools is evident in table 1, which describes each of the schools in the Chicago sample in terms of basic demographic characteristics.

Within each school, two first-grade and two fifth-grade classrooms were selected to participate in the study, yielding a final sample of twenty classrooms at each of the two grade levels in Sendai and Taipei and forty at each grade level in Chicago. The classrooms were chosen in consultation with the principal of the school to be representative of the population of students at each grade level. If the teacher refused to participate in the study—a rare event—a different classroom was selected. Within each classroom in the American sample, all children whose parents returned permission slips and who were present on the day of testing were tested on the group tests. The median percentage of students tested in each American classroom was 94. In Sendai and Taipei, permission of the principal and teachers was sufficient for including a child in our study, and all students in each of the Chinese and Japanese classrooms who were present on the day of testing

Table 1
Characteristics of the Schools in the Chicago Sample

School Number	Location	Public or Private	Grade Levels	Number of Students	Ethnic Composition (in percent)				
					Black	White	Hispanic	Asian	Other
1	City	Public	1-8	1182	91.4	4.6	2.0	0.0	2.0
2	City	Public	K-8	886	3.2	54.8	11.1	25.4	5.6
3	City	Public	P-8	700	100.0	0.0	0.0	0.0	0.0
4	City	Public	P-8	1049	0.0	64.9	21.6	2.9	10.5
5	City	Public	K-8	1133	100.0	0.0	0.0	0.0	0.0
6	City	Public	P-8	1402	0.0	33.7	66.3	0.0	0.0
7	City	Public	P, 3-8	798	100.0	0.0	0.0	0.0	0.0
8	City	Public	P-8	1446	0.7	12.4	85.0	0.0	2.0
9	City	Public	P-5	875	33.3	21.1	29.8	11.4	4.4
10	County	Public	K-3, 7-8	610	0.0	62.1	35.7	0.7	1.4
11	County	Public	Jr.K-5	303	0.0	97.9	0.0	2.1	0.0
12	County	Public	E.C.-6	550	0.0	99.2	0.8	0.0	0.0
13	County	Public	K-5	317	9.3	82.9	2.3	5.4	0.0
14	County	Public	K-5	320	0.0	79.8	1.7	16.8	1.7
15	County	Public	K-6	350	0.0	97.6	0.8	1.6	0.0
16	County	Private	K-8	516	0.0	100.0	0.0	0.0	0.0
17	City	Private	P-8	950	0.0	99.3	0.0	0.7	0.0
18	City	Private	K-8	635	0.5	59.5	24.7	11.1	4.2
19	City	Private	K-8	437	0.0	99.3	0.7	0.0	0.0
20	County	Private	P-8	594	0.0	100.0	0.0	0.0	0.0

were tested. The final sample for the group testing consisted of 5524 students: 750 first-grade and 808 fifth-grade students in Sendai; 1037 and 954 in Taipei; and 976 and 999 in Chicago.

The average age of the children at time of testing was 80.6, 78.6, and 76.0 months for the Japanese, Chinese, and American first graders and 128.8, 127.0, and 126.5 months for the Japanese, Chinese, and American fifth graders, respectively. The mean number of years of mothers' and fathers' education was 12.5 and 13.6 in Sendai for first and fifth graders, respectively, 10.8 and 12.3 in Taipei, and 12.9 and 13.6 in Chicago.

Examiners. All testing was conducted by examiners who were residents of the cities in which the research was conducted. In Sendai, examiners were students in social work and psychology at Tohoku Fukushi University. In Taipei, examiners were drawn from teacher-training programs at Taipei Teachers College. Examiners in Chicago were graduate and undergraduate students from education, behavioral sciences, and social work programs at the University of Chicago and other Chicago colleges. Examiners were carefully trained, and their knowledge of the testing procedures was thoroughly checked before they were sent into the schools.

Procedure. Children in each classroom were tested by a team consisting of a chief examiner and from two to six monitors, depending on the grade and size of the classrooms. Each child was given a test booklet (reproduced in Appendix A) and was told not to begin work until instructed to do so by the chief examiner. The chief examiner then read aloud the general instructions and answered questions from the students. The monitors on the team spread out around the classroom so that they could make sure that all children were working on the correct page of the test booklet. They also assisted children who appeared not to understand the instructions.

In first-grade classrooms, instructions for the first fifteen items on the test were read aloud by the chief examiner. After each question was read, the monitors in the room checked to see that each child was answering the question in the correct place on the answer sheet. After the monitors indicated that all students had answered a given question, the next question was read. After the class had completed the first fifteen questions, the examiner read the following instructions:

> There are some more questions. These questions are for older children, so many of them may be too difficult for you. Just do as many as you can. When you get to the pink page, close your booklet and put your pencil on the desk. You can start now.

Children worked independently on the remaining items for a maximum of twenty minutes.

For fifth graders, only the general instructions were read; then students worked independently during the twenty minutes allowed for the test.

Results

Means and standard deviations of scores on the computation test for each city and grade are presented in table 2. Analyses of variance revealed highly significant differences among the scores for the three cities at both grade levels, F's $(2, 2727–2733) = 262.83–1230.27$, p's $< .001$, but no significant differences by sex or interactions between city and sex. The American students received significantly lower scores than the Japanese and Chinese students at both grade levels, but the difference is much greater at fifth grade than at first grade.

Classification by subsets of items. The computation test included a wide variety of items. To gain a more detailed view of the computational skills tested, we have divided the items into eight topic groups: basic number concepts, addition and subtraction of whole numbers, multiplication and division of whole numbers, the concept of fractions, addition and subtraction of fractions, multiplication and division of fractions, addition and subtraction of decimals, and multiplication and division of decimals.

The relative performance of children in each city is most evident if the results are measured on a common scale. We followed a four-step procedure to accomplish this purpose. First, we found the distribution of scores at

Table 2
Average Scores on Group Computation Test by City and Grade

City and Grade	N	Mean	SD
First Grade			
Sendai	750	16.4	2.5
Taipei	1037	15.6	3.5
Chicago	976	13.0	3.6
Fifth Grade			
Sendai	808	56.7	5.8
Taipei	954	57.7	4.7
Chicago	999	45.7	6.6

each grade for each subscale, combining the scores for all three cities. Second, we assigned each child a standard (z) score on the basis of his or her status in this distribution. Third, we obtained an average z-score for the children in each city. Finally, an adjustment for sample size was made to the mean z-scores for each city by adding a constant so that the mean of the three city-means would be equal to zero. The mean z-scores for each city, adjusted for cross-national differences in sample size, are presented in figure 1. It is clear from figure 1 that the relatively low performance of the American children relative to the Asian children is pervasive, occurring in all topics tested.

Partitioning of variance. Because we first sampled schools, then classrooms within schools, and finally children within classrooms, the variability in test scores could be derived from any or all of these three sources. Further, it is possible that the amount of variance due to each source differs

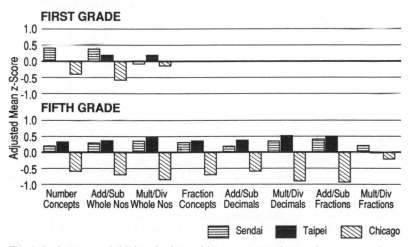

Fig. 1. Performance of children in three cities on computation test items grouped according to topic

among the three cities. To understand the sources of variability within each city, we used statistical procedures for partitioning the variance into that due to schools, classrooms within schools, and individuals within classrooms.[1]

The results of this analysis are presented in figure 2 by city and grade. The total height of the bar for each city represents the total variance, and the regions of each bar represent variance due to the different sources. Several interesting findings are evident. Overall variability in the American sample is greater than that in either Taipei or Sendai at both grade levels. In addition, the source of the variability differs markedly between Chicago on the one hand and Taipei and Sendai on the other. At both grade levels, almost all the variance in Sendai and Taipei is found at the level of individuals within classrooms, with little, if any, variance resulting from differences among classrooms within schools or from differences among schools. In the Chicago sample, a different picture emerges. Although more than half the variance in Chicago is attributable to individual variability within classrooms, there is also a sizeable portion of variance attributable to differences

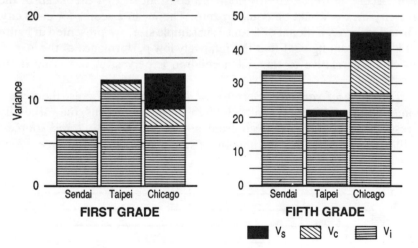

Fig. 2. Variance on the computation test partitioned among schools, classrooms, and individuals, for each city

1. Variances due to school (V_s), class (V_c), and individual (V_i) were computed as follows (MS = Mean Square; SS = Sum of Squares):

$$V_s = [MS_{school} - MS_{class}]/N \text{ of students per school}$$
$$V_c = [MS_{class} - MS_{individual}]/N \text{ of students per class}$$
$$V_i = MS_{individual}$$

where MS_{school} was the $MS_{between}$ that resulted from a one-way ANOVA with school as the independent variable and individual computation test scores as the dependent variable; $MS_{individual}$ was the MS_{error} that resulted from a one-way ANOVA of the same scores, but with classroom as the independent variable; and MS_{class} was calculated as $MS_{class} = [SS_{class} - SS_{school}]/[\text{total } N \text{ of classes} - \text{total } N \text{ of schools}]$. We are grateful to David A. Kenny for suggesting this method of partitioning variances.

among classrooms and differences among schools. If we look only at variability among individuals within classrooms, Chicago does not differ markedly from the other two cities. In fact, variability among individuals in Chicago classrooms lies midway between Sendai and Taipei at both grade levels. Finally, in both Sendai and Chicago, variability tended to increase between first and fifth grades; in Taipei, variability declined. These data make it difficult to argue, as some have done, that one of the major problems of teaching mathematics in American classrooms compared to Asian classrooms is the great heterogeneity in levels of ability among children in American classrooms.

Discussion

The results obtained from the group testing of computational skills replicates the pattern of results obtained in our earlier study (Stevenson, Lee, and Stigler 1986; Stigler et al. (1982). By first grade, students in Japan and Taiwan are already ahead of their U.S. counterparts, although there is some overlap in the distribution of scores. By fifth grade, the difference has widened dramatically.

But computational skills such as those evaluated in this test encompass only part of what elementary school students need to learn about mathematics. Mastering arithmetic is important, but they also need to be able to apply this knowledge to the solution of quantitative problems. The possibility that American children's deficit in computational abilities is not accompanied by an early deficit in meeting the higher-level goals of the mathematics curriculum, such as problem solving, was assesssed in the battery of individual tests.

INDIVIDUAL TESTING:
PROBLEM SOLVING AND BEYOND

Method

Sampling. It was impossible to conduct two hours of individual testing with each of the more than 5000 students in the classrooms visited. Thus, we chose a subsample of children to represent the eighty classrooms at each grade. We randomly chose three girls and three boys from each classroom, resulting in subsamples, at each grade, of 120 children in Taipei and Sendai and 240 children in Chicago.

One of the first questions that can be asked about the subsamples is how representative they were of the total samples. In figure 3, we present graphic representations of the distributions of scores on the group computation test for the full sample and for the subsample in each city at each grade. It is obvious that the distributions of scores for the subsamples closely resemble

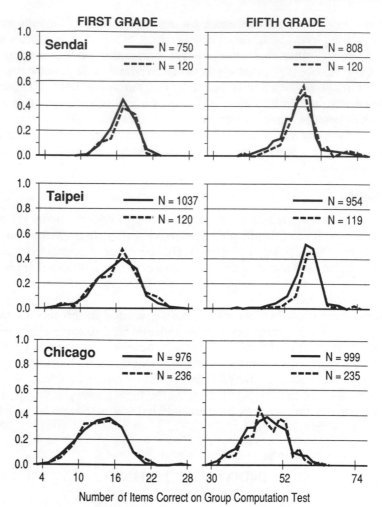

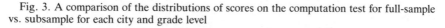

Number of Items Correct on Group Computation Test

Fig. 3. A comparison of the distributions of scores on the computation test for full-sample vs. subsample for each city and grade level

those for the full samples. Although there was slightly less variability within the subsample than in the full sample (as would be expected by chance), a comparison of the full-sample and subsample means for each city and grade reveals that the subsample means differ from the full-sample means by an average of only one-eighth of a standard deviation. In addition, this difference in means was generally in the same direction (i.e., the subsample means were slightly higher than the full-sample means). We conclude that the subsamples used in the individual testing adequately represent the full sample.

Description of Tests. One major goal in constructing the battery of tests was to include problems of the types found in the mathematics curricula.

We also included problems that were indirectly related to the goals of the curriculum.

The tests given at both grades included word problems, concepts and equations, estimation, operations, graphing, visualization, mental folding, and mental calculation. In addition, first graders were given an oral test of reasoning and fifth graders were given a geometry test. The geometry test was administered as a group test immediately after the computation test but will be discussed with the individual tests, since it fits better there conceptually. The content of the individual tests appears in Appendix B. A brief description of each test is provided here.

Word problems consisted of twenty-seven problems ranging in level of difficulty from kindergarten to seventh grade. First and fifth graders all started with the first problem and continued until they missed a specified number of problems. The problems were challenging and diverse and included some beyond the level of complexity found in elementary school textbooks.

The number concepts and equations section was designed to probe children's understanding of some of the basic concepts of the mathematics curriculum. The first-grade test contained thirty-four questions; the fifth-grade test, thirty-one. Major topics at both grade levels included the concepts of place value and negative numbers and the meaning of equations. In addition, first graders were tested on their understanding of counting and fifth graders on their understanding of fractions.

Estimation was one of two tests that assessed children's abilities to map numbers and arithmetical operations onto real-world objects and events. In this test children estimated the answers to questions involving number and quantity. For example, given a line whose endpoints were labeled with numbers, children were asked to assign a number to a third point on the line. Or, children were asked to estimate the number of dots in a random configuration that was shown for three seconds.

Operations problems consisted of eight questions for first graders and eight for fifth graders. Four questions at each grade level measured the child's ability to map arithmetic operations onto the world, and four measured the ability to verbalize the uses of operations.

It is generally recognized that visual and spatial skills play an important role in mathematical problem solving. Some of these skills, such as solving geometry problems and interpreting the graphic presentation of data, are taught as part of the mathematics curriculum. Others, such as the mental transformation of visual images, are not taught. Both types of visual skills were assessed in a series of four tests.

Geometry contained seventeen items. Some items assessed children's vocabulary of geometric terms, such as *square* and *trapezoid*. In other questions children were asked to find the areas of two-dimensional figures or the missing dimensions of various circles and triangles.

Graphing was intended to assess how well children could extract information from conventional tabular or graphic representations of data.

Visualization and *Mental folding* consisted of novel problems aimed at assessing children's visual problem-solving skills. The visualization test included twelve items that required the child to encode pictures and mentally transform them to solve the problem. For example, one item presented three drawings of coiled rope and asked whether pulling the ends of each rope would form a knot. The mental folding test consisted of ten problems in which children were asked to follow mentally a set of verbal instructions involving a series of folds of two-dimensional figures.

Mental calculation contained four parts. First-grade students did only part A; fifth graders did all four parts. In part A, children were given one minute to solve single-digit addition problems. In part B, the problems involved adding two two-digit numbers. In part C, two-digit numbers were to be multiplied by a one-digit number. Part D consisted of five untimed problems involving two- and three-digit numbers that children were asked to solve mentally.

Oral problems contained six "trick" problems that did not require computation. Rather, they tapped children's reasoning ability about quantity, frequency, ordinal position, and other fundamental mathematical concepts. For example, one problem stated, "There were 3 apples and 2 pears on a plate. The children ate all the fruit for lunch. How many pears were left on the plate?"

Procedure. The tests were administered to children on two consecutive days. On the first day, the tests were word problems, operations, visualization, and graphing. On the second day, the tests were oral problems (first grade only), mental calculation, number concepts and equations, estimation, and mental folding. The tests were administered in the order listed.

The materials were a booklet of visual materials that was shown to the child, a booklet containing instructions read by the examiner, and a data sheet on which the child's responses were recorded.

Individual testing was conducted in a separate room within the school. The examiner put the child at ease and began testing after several minutes. The examiner made sure that the children understood the problems and that possible difficulties in reading would not affect the children's performance. The examiner read each problem to the child, who answered orally. Even the word problems, which were printed in large type in the booklet of visual materials, were read aloud to the child. Children were told that they could ask to have a problem repeated at any time. They were allowed to use paper and pencil if they wished, and the printed version of each problem remained in front of the child as the child attempted to solve it.

Overview of Results

The total number of correct items on each test was determined for each child. Items that could not be scored this way are discussed in detail below. However, first we would like to present an overview of the cross-cultural results.

The relative performance of children in each city is most evident if the results are measured on a common scale. In order to accomplish this, we followed the same four-step procedure used before to compute z-scores for each subscale of the computation test. The mean z-scores for each city and grade, adjusted for differences in sample size, are presented in figure 4.

The overall trends are readily evident. The means for Japanese students are the highest; those for the American students, the lowest. Chinese students generally fall between the Japanese and U.S. means. The status of the Japanese students remains relatively constant across grade levels. However, between first and fifth grades, the relative status of the American children shows a striking decline and the performance of Chinese students shows remarkable improvement. The conclusion is clear. Asian children's high level of performance in mathematics is not restricted to a narrow range of well-rehearsed, automatic computational skills but is manifest across a wide range of tasks and problems. Analyses of variance revealed that means for the cities differed significantly on every test, F's $(2, 468) = 10.2–856.5$, p's $< .001$. Few differences by sex were found, and there were no significant interactions between city and sex.

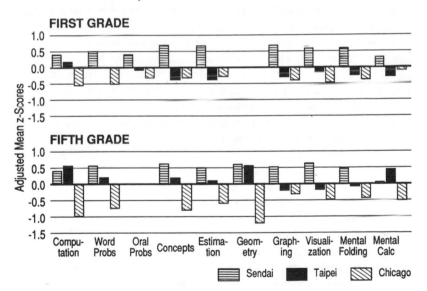

Fig. 4. Mean performance of children in three cities on the individual mathematics tests

Knowledge Differences in More Detail

In addition to overall differences in performance, more detailed analyses reveal other cross-cultural differences. Our intent is not to be exhaustive but to illustrate the kinds of differences that were found. Detailed data for all test items may be found in Appendix B.

Word problems. Word problems were easy for Japanese students. It is interesting to speculate about why this should be, especially given the difficulty American children have in solving such problems (Carpenter and Moser 1983; Riley, Greeno, and Heller 1983). On the basis of our observations of classrooms in the three cultures, we have found that word problems are an integral part of mathematics lessons in both Japan and Taiwan (Stigler and Perry 1988) but are rarely taught in U.S. classrooms, where they tend, instead, to be used as homework problems to be done for practice. Furthermore, the way word problems are presented in U.S. textbooks obviates the need for children to attend closely to the problems. Rather than presenting diverse types of problems, U.S. textbooks take the simplest kind of word problem and present it many times in a row, changing only the numbers and the content (Stigler, et al. 1986). Children quickly learn in these circumstances to focus on key words that help them decide which operation to use on the numbers in the problem. Once they have determined which operation to use, they seem to abandon further efforts at analysis.

An examination of children's performance on the oral problems sheds some light on the sources of the American children's difficulties. An analysis of the types of errors that children produced in the three cultures is especially informative. Correct response to the oral problems did not require calculation. In fact, the child was incorrect if he or she tried to perform a calculation using the numbers given in the problem. In view of the stereotyped way word problems are taught in U.S. classrooms, we might expect American children to err by performing a calculation when none was required, whereas Japanese students might be more likely to respond "don't know" or produce some other type of error.

In order to see if there were cultural differences in the kinds of errors produced on the oral problems, all incorrect answers were coded into three categories: (1) calculation (i.e., the answer was the sum, difference, or product of the numbers in the problem); (2) "don't know"; or (3) other kinds of errors. The relative frequencies of these errors, together with the frequency of correct responses, are shown in figure 5. Because only five of the six problems could be coded in this way, the number of responses in each category could range from 0 to 5. As we saw in figure 4, the number of correct responses was highest in Sendai, next highest in Taipei, and lowest in Chicago. In the category coded "other," the highest frequency occurred in Chicago, and the lowest in Sendai.

Children in Sendai performed the smallest number of calculations in responding to the problems but were most likely to say they did not know. In both Taipei and Chicago the reverse was true, that is, calculations were

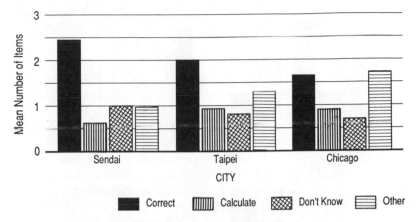

Fig. 5. Types of responses by first graders in three cities to the oral reasoning test

more frequent than "don't know's." This interaction was statistically significant, $F(2, 469) = 5.5, p < .01$.

These data suggest that American and Chinese children tend to compute first and think later. Japanese students are taught differently, and the effects show up in their responses on the oral problems. Rather than approach each problem with ritualistic efforts at calculation, they were more likely to evaluate whether or not they could make a correct reply.

Quantifying the world. A series of items in the estimation test assessed children's abilities to assign numbers to objects. These items required a knowledge of numbers that includes a sense of quantity with respect to dimensions like length and numerosity. To be literate in mathematics, one needs to know not only that 450 is more than 45 but also that a certain group of objects is closer to 45 than to 450 in number.

Four types of items are of special interest. In the first type, children were shown a drawing of an object and a unit with which to measure the object. They were asked to look at the drawing and estimate the number of units required to span the object. In the second type, children were shown an unmarked number line with the two endpoints labeled and asked to assign a number to a target point marked with an "x" on the line. (These items were scored correct if the students' answer was within plus or minus 10 percent of the numerical length of the line.) In the third type, children were shown three line segments and asked to pick the one of a specified length. Finally, children were shown a random configuration of dots for three seconds and asked to choose their estimate of the total number of dots in the display from four alternatives.

The mean percentage of students in each city who answered each type of item correctly appears in figure 6. City by sex analyses of variance revealed significant main effects of city for every subscale at both grade levels, all p's

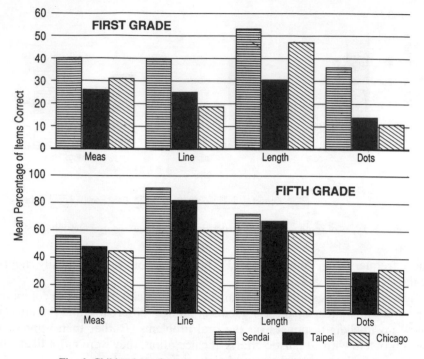

Fig. 6. Children's performance on four parts of the estimation test

< .001, except for dots in grade 5, where p < .05. There were no significant effects of sex and no significant interactions. Japanese students generally did the best and the American students the worst. There was one exception: American first graders did better than the Chinese first graders in judging length. Perhaps the most remarkable feature of these results is the large difference on the dots task at first grade, where the Japanese children were superior to both the Chinese and American children. The task requiring students to assign numbers to points on a number line became more difficult as the numerical length of the line increased (i.e., estimating distances was more difficult on the line running from 1 to 100 than on the line running from 0 to 10) and when larger numbers were used to label the endpoints (i.e., the most difficult line was the one running from 500 to 700). Figure 7 shows the percentage of fifth graders who got each of the four items on this task correct. American children had great difficulty in handling large numbers. There was only a modest decline in the incidence of correct response for Chinese and Japanese children as the size of the numbers increased, but there was a precipitous drop for the American children.

Real-world associations of arithmetic operations. In the typical word problem, students are asked to analyze a verbally presented real-world problem and generate a mathematical solution. In the arithmetic operations task,

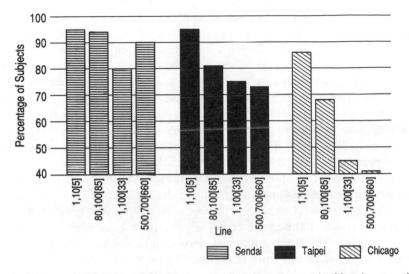

Fig. 7. Percentage of fifth-grade students responding correctly to each of four items on the line estimation task (on *x* axis, the first two numbers indicate how the endpoints were labeled; the number in brackets is the correct answer)

students were asked to do the opposite: given a mathematical formulation, could they generate a real-world situation to which the formulation could be applied?

For example, both first- and fifth-grade students were given a simple equation (e.g., $5 + 2 = ?$) and asked to make up a word problem to fit the equation. Among Japanese first graders, 79 percent responded with a valid story problem, compared to only 39 percent of Chinese and 44 percent of American first graders. By fifth grade, the Japanese percentage had risen slightly to 86, and the Chinese percentage to 85, but the American percentage was only 60.

At first grade, 13 percent of United States children and 11 percent of Chinese children responded with a completely numerical problem, such as "What's 4 and 3?" or "5 minus 2." Only 2 percent of Japanese children responded this way.

Further insight into the children's ability to generate applications of arithmetic operations can be found in their responses to "Martian" problems, such as, "Pretend that some Martians came to visit you, and they had never heard of addition. If they asked you to tell them all the ways you could use addition, what would you tell them?" There were many ways to code the responses to these questions.

One way that children could respond was to generate a specific example of a problem that could be solved using the operation under discussion. This strategy was chosen by more than half the children in each city. However, the kinds of examples differed among the three cities. Examples were assigned to one of two categories: (*a*) story problems (e.g., "There were 3 books and 1 was lost; how many were left?"), or (*b*) number problems (e.g., "What's 3 − 1?"). Story problems indicated that children were mapping the operation onto the world, whereas the usefulness of number problems was confined to arithmetic itself. Of Japanese first-grade children who gave an example, 79 percent generated story problems and 21 percent constructed number problems. The pattern in Taiwan was similar: 72 percent story problems and 28 percent number problems. In Chicago, the reverse occurred: only 21 percent of Chicago first graders generated story problems, and 79 percent generated number problems. In fifth grade, the percentage of children generating story problems increased somewhat, but the difference between the Asian and American children remained. The percentage of fifth graders generating story problems versus those who generated number problems was 100 percent versus 0 percent in Sendai and 91 percent versus 9 percent in Taipei. Among American fifth graders, only 63 percent of the examples were story problems, and 37 percent were number problems.

A less common type of response to the Martian problems (produced by about 20 percent of the children in all three cities) was to refer to a domain of application; for example, "Use it to count money" or "Use it when you go shopping." Some of the responses, like those given as examples, referred to real-world domains; others referred to real-world Martian domains (e.g., "Use it to count your spaceships"); and still others referred to school (e.g., "Use it on tests" or "To get an A on your report card").

An analysis was made of the percentage of children who referred to real-world or Martian domains versus those who referred to school. At first grade, 51 percent of Japanese students who gave this type of response referred to real-world or Martian domains, whereas 81 percent of Chinese and 44 percent of U.S. students did so. The remaining children, 49 percent of Japanese, 19 percent of Chinese, and 56 percent of American children, referred only to school as the domain in which the operation could be used. By fifth grade, students in all cities referred to the real world in the majority of their responses, yet there was still a cross-national difference. The real world (or the Martian world) was referred to by 92 percent of Japanese and 87 percent of Chinese fifth graders but by only 76 percent of American fifth graders. Conversely, only 8 percent of Japanese and 13 percent of Chinese fifth graders referred to school as the domain in which arithmetic operations were most useful, whereas 24 percent of U.S. students did.

It is evident in the children's replies that the Asian children view mathematics as relevant to the real world and generate real-world situations to which mathematics can be applied. American children more frequently regard mathematics as restricted and fail to see the relationship between mathematics and real-world problems.

Operations and equations. A particularly striking deficiency evidenced by U.S. students was their lack of ability to interpret the correct meanings of mathematical equations. First graders, for example, were shown four problems: $6 - 2$, $3 + 4$, $8 \div 2$, and 3×5. For each problem they were asked simply to identify the problem as addition, subtraction, multiplication, or division. Their answers are summarized in figure 8. Since first-grade children have studied addition and subtraction, they should have had little difficulty with those terms. However, this expectation proved valid only for Japanese and Chinese children. American children had difficulty, and fewer than 65 percent of the children correctly identified $3 + 4$ as an addition problem. For multiplication and division neither American nor Chinese children did well; under 40 percent responded correctly. Japanese children did better, showing greater awareness of these mathematical concepts than American or Chinese children.

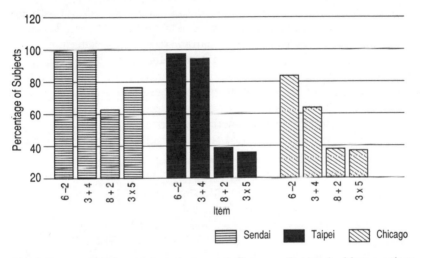

Fig. 8. Percentage of first-grade students responding correctly to each of four questions asking, "Is this problem addition, subtraction, multiplication, or division?"

A series of more complex questions concerning a knowledge of equations appeared at fifth grade. Three of these items are presented in table 3, along with the percentage of fifth-grade students in each location who responded correctly. Since it seems unlikely that the problems posed computational

Table 3
Percentages of Fifth Graders in Sendai, Taipei, and Chicago Responding Correctly to Selected Questions Using Equations

Item	Sendai	Taipei	Chicago
$4 + 6 + 3 = \underline{\quad} + 3$	90	85	39
$(4 + 5) + 2 = 4 + \underline{\quad}$	88	90	42
$8 \times 7 = 7 \times \underline{\quad}$	97	99	71

difficulties, the poor performance of U.S. children is probably attributable to a lack of understanding of the equal sign (=) in the context of equations.

Graphing and visualization. In observing Japanese classrooms, one is struck by the heavy reliance on visual representations of mathematical concepts. Not only are visual representations used by teachers in explaining concepts, but the children themselves are expected to become competent at drawing, for example, geometric figures in three-dimensional perspective. Thus, it is not surprising that Japanese children do well on tests involving visualization. Three of our tests had this focus: graphing, visualization, and mental folding. It is clear in figure 4 that the pattern of performance across cities was similar on all three tests. Japanese children did extremely well and American children did very badly. Scores for the Chinese children were only slightly higher than those of the American children.

The graphing test exemplifies this trend. In this test children were given information in tables, line graphs, bar graphs, and (for fifth grade only) pie graphs and were asked to read information from the presentations. Performance is classified by type of presentation in figure 9.

Figure 9 shows the clear superiority of Japanese children in the interpretation of all types of tables and graphs. Chinese and American children's performances were similar to each other, and poor.

Lessons on graphing appear in the mathematics curricula of all three countries. However, the pattern of results for graphing evident in figure 9

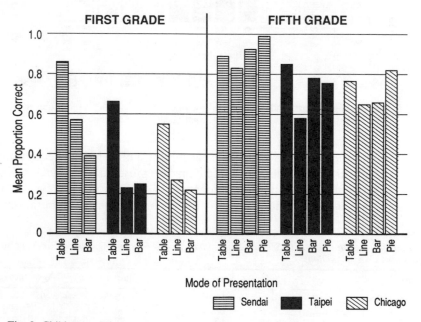

Fig. 9. Children's performance on subparts of the graphing test, by city and grade level

also appears in the test of mental folding, a skill that is not directly taught in school. In figure 10, we have plotted the performance of children in each city on the ten items of the mental folding test. For ease of interpretation we plotted the items in order of their difficulty across the three locations. Although performance in all three cities improved between first and fifth grade, the Japanese are superior at both grade levels. Again, the curves for Chinese and American children are similar.

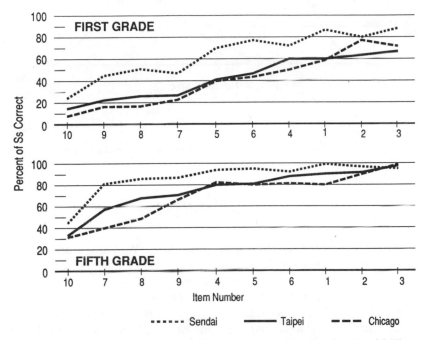

Fig. 10. Percentage of students responding correctly to each item on the mental folding test (items at each grade level are arranged in order of difficulty

Geometry. Basic concepts of geometry are emphasized far more strongly in both Japanese and Chinese textbooks than they are in U.S. textbooks. This emphasis is evident in the results of the geometry test. Distributions of fifth graders' scores on the group geometry test are presented in figure 11 for the children in each city. In the graph we have plotted the proportion of cases with each number correct divided by the sample standard deviation, as recommended by Freedman, Pisani, and Purves (1980). The distributions of scores are relatively normal. However, there are large mean differences between the scores in Chicago and in the other two cities. Analysis of variance confirmed a highly significant effect of city, $F(2, 468) = 856.5$, $p < .001$, but no significant effect of sex and no significant interaction. Scores for the Chicago fifth graders were much lower than those in Sendai and

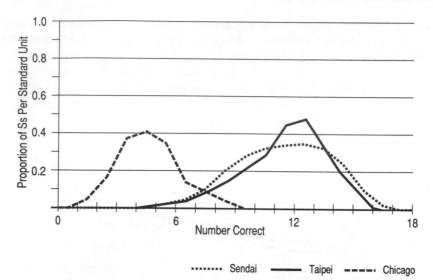

Fig. 11. Frequency polygon of fifth graders' scores on the group geometry test (means for each city—Sendai, 10.9; Taipei, 10.9; Chicago, 4.3)

Taipei, p's < .001, but the difference between Sendai and Taipei was not significant.

Place value and the problem of large numbers. We know from previous analyses of the elementary mathematics curricula in Japan, Taiwan, and the United States that U.S. curricula tend to avoid dealing with large numbers until the later grades of elementary school. Japanese and Chinese curricula, in contrast, introduce large numbers early and practice each new computational skill with problems that use both large and small numbers (Fuson, Stigler, and Bartsch 1988). Various items throughout our battery of tests indicate that these differences in curricular emphasis do affect children's knowledge.

First graders were presented with the numerals 10032, 132, and 32, and asked which one shows the number "one hundred thirty-two." In Sendai, 70 percent of the children answered correctly, compared to 38 percent in Taipei and 25 percent in Chicago. Fifth graders were asked to read the following numbers: 498, 800070, and 20350076. Most children could read the first one (100 percent in Sendai, 97 percent in Taipei, and 98 percent in Chicago); however, the U.S. children fell behind with the larger numbers. The number 800070 was read correctly by 96 percent of fifth graders in Sendai, 90 percent in Taipei, but only 53 percent in Chicago. Similarly, the number 20350076 was read correctly by 96 percent of fifth graders in Sendai, 76 percent in Taipei, and only 45 percent in Chicago.

Several items indicated that American fifth graders have particular difficulties even with simple computations when they are embedded in the context of larger, multidigit numbers. In one series of questions, children were asked to solve 5 + 7, 50 + 70, 500 + 700, and 500 + 70. In another, similar series, they were asked to solve 3 × 6, 30 × 60, and 300 × 600. The percentage of students in each city responding correctly to each question is presented in figure 12. Although U.S. children do almost as well as children in the other locations in answering the first question in each series, their performance falls after that, diverging from the pattern of results in both Japan and Taiwan.

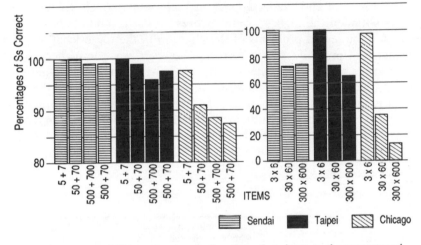

Fig. 12. Percentage of fifth graders responding correctly to items on the concepts and equations test

Time. One of the most striking features of elementary mathematics classrooms in Taiwan is the emphasis placed on rapid retrieval of arithmetic facts. There is daily practice through tests of mental calculation. Japanese teachers, by contrast, stress the importance of thinking about and evaluating alternative strategies for solving problems, and their pace is slower and more relaxed. American classrooms generally are fast paced, but there is not a conscious emphasis on the importance of speed. Rather, the pace of United States classrooms appears to be dictated by the need to "get through the material."

It is evident in figure 4 that the Chinese emphasis on speed in mental calculation pays off by the time children are in the fifth grade. In fact, the speed tests were the one area in which Chinese children consistently outperformed Japanese children. In our fifth-grade sample, Chinese students correctly solved an average of 14.4 mental additions of two two-digit numbers in sixty seconds, compared to 12.2 for Japanese students and 7.8 for U.S. students. At fifth grade, the numbers of two-digit by one-digit problems multiplied mentally in sixty seconds were 7.7 for Chinese, 5.8 for Japanese, and 4.0 for American students. Chinese students, even under time pressure, excelled in their ability to produce the correct answer to arithmetic problems quickly.

The Japanese de-emphasis on speed of performance is accompanied by a strong emphasis on thoughtful reflection and the importance of executing procedures carefully and correctly. One consequence of these attitudes was revealed in a further analysis of data from the group computation test. We looked at how many problems each child attempted within the twenty minutes and the percentage of those attempted that were solved correctly. These analyses, by city and grade, appear in table 4. Although Japanese first graders obtained the highest overall scores on the computation test, they attempted the fewest problems of the children in the three locations. The percentage of problems solved correctly, however, was the highest: nearly 85 percent of the problems attempted were solved correctly by children in Sendai. Chicago first graders were correct on only 61 percent of the problems they attempted. In fifth grade, the pattern is similar except that both the Chinese and Japanese students correctly solved around 77 percent of the problems attempted, compared to only 51 percent of the American students.

Table 4
Number of Problems Attempted and Percentage Correct on Computation Test, by City and Grade

City and Grade	Mean Number of Problems Attempted	Mean Percentage Solved Correctly
First Grade		
Sendai	19.5	84.7
Taipei	21.5	74.6
Chicago	22.4	60.7
Fifth Grade		
Sendai	37.9	76.5
Taipei	39.2	76.8
Chicago	36.1	50.7

The slow pace of Japanese students in approaching problem solving is further indicated in the time taken to complete the individual tests that contained a fixed number of problems. There were four such tasks at first grade and three at fifth grade. The average times in minutes taken to complete the tasks are presented in figure 13. The same pattern appeared at both grades. Japanese students consistently took the most time to complete the tasks and Chinese students took the least. City by sex analyses of variance indicated that the cross-cultural differences were statistically significant at both grade levels, F's $= 29.4–242.0$, p's $< .001$.

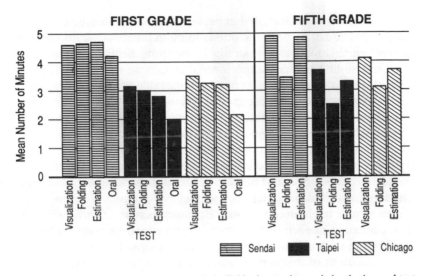

Fig. 13. Length of time students took to do individual tests, by grade level, city, and test

GENERAL DISCUSSION

Our primary purpose in this study was to identify differences in the mathematical knowledge of Chinese, Japanese, and American children and to analyze characteristic approaches of these children to the solution of problems in mathematics. We have not focused here on explanations of why there should be such remarkable differences in mathematics achievement, since we have attempted to do that in other publications (Stevenson et al. 1990; Stevenson et al. in press; Stigler and Perry 1988).

The deficiencies displayed by the American children were more serious than we expected. There was no area in which they were competitive with the children from Japan and Taiwan, whether in computation, speed, or the application of mathematical principles. With problems as diverse as estimating the distance between a tree and a hidden treasure on a map, deciding who won a race on the basis of data in a graph, trying to explain subtraction to visiting Martians, or calculating the sum of 19 and 45, significantly fewer American than Chinese or Japanese children solved the problems correctly. The situation did not improve between the first and fifth grades. Indeed, the status of the American children relative to the Chinese and Japanese children deteriorated, while the status of the Chinese children improved. Japanese children maintained their superiority at both grades.

As has been shown in earlier comparative studies, Japanese students excel in mathematics. In our study, they were notable both for the pervasiveness of their skills and knowledge and for the early age at which these become evident. Taiwan was not included in previous comparative studies, and only in the recent IEA study were the outstanding mathematics skills of Chinese students—in this instance, students from Hong Kong—evident. In our study, Chinese first graders outperformed American first graders, but they did not display a level of achievement comparable to that of the Japanese children. However, the Chinese children showed remarkable improvement and by the fifth grade were well on their way to attaining a level of performance equal to that of the Japanese children.

A concern often expressed about cross-cultural studies is the comparability of the samples of subjects in the different cultures and of the content of the tests used. We followed the same procedure for obtaining our samples of children in each of the cities, and we believe our goal of testing a representative sample of children was met. Because there is universal elementary school education in each of the three locations and because participation by children in each city was high, the samples should be as representative of the populations of children in each city as it is possible to obtain.

Our use of curriculum-based tests avoided the problem often found in cross-cultural research of constructing instruments in one culture and language and then translating them for use in other cultures. By collaborating with colleagues from Taiwan and Japan in the construction of the tests and by basing the tests on analyses of the textbooks used in each culture, we avoided the possibility that the tests were culturally biased or irrelevant to the actual curriculum to which children in each culture were exposed. Other tests in our battery tapped important components of mathematical knowledge that were not directly taught in school. The pattern of results was the same, whether the tests were derived directly from the curricula or required answers to novel questions, such as estimating the number of dots on a page or visualizing spatial transformations of line drawings.

It is sometimes suggested that it is more difficult to accommodate the needs of American children than of Chinese and Japanese children because of the greater heterogeneity of students in American classrooms. This interpretation was not supported in the present study. The American teachers were not faced with a broader array of skill and knowledge among their students than the Chinese and Japanese teachers were. Although the variability of scores was greater in the American than in the Chinese and Japanese samples, this was not due to greater differences in children's scores within the American classrooms. Rather, the greater variability of the American scores was derived from greater variability among classrooms and among schools.

Two factors may account for the greater variability among classrooms and among schools in the United States. First, there is no national curriculum, as in Taiwan and Japan, that defines the content and even the pace of what is taught in elementary school classrooms. Second, there is frequent segregation by socioeconomic class and ethnic group in large American cities, whereas neighborhoods tend to be similar to each other in large Asian cities.

We find little merit to the argument that Asian students acquire their skills in mathematics through rote learning and that they excel primarily in the solution of problems that depend on automatic, routinized solutions. They did display skill in computation, but more impressive was their performance in tasks that required an understanding of the structure and operations of mathematics. In fact, it was the American children who tended to approach problems in a stereotyped manner. For example, when presented with problems that required reasoning rather than calculation, American children were much more likely than Chinese or Japanese children to try to solve the problem by calculation—a routinized procedure they had learned to apply to mathematics problems.

One advantage that Chinese and Japanese children may have over Western children lies in the Chinese and Japanese counting systems. The facility with which these children were able to handle large numbers in problems involving computation, recognition, or estimation may be due to the fact that there are single terms denoting units such as ten thousand as well as, thousands, hundreds, and tens in both the Chinese and Japanese languages. The construction of large numbers may be more evident by this counting system than by systems that do not involve reducing large numbers to defined subunits. Moreover, as was pointed out, American teachers and textbook writers are more reluctant than Chinese or Japanese to introduce large numbers into the children's mathematics curricula. American children are thereby deprived of opportunities to practice reading and using large numbers in their early mathematics lessons.

American children displayed difficulty in relating their knowledge of mathematics to the real world. This is not surprising when one examines the way American children are taught mathematics. As part of our study we observed each classroom for four hours. The results of these observations will be presented elsewhere, but two features are especially relevant here. The frequency with which teachers gave children real-world problems and used concrete, manipulable objects in their teaching differed greatly among the three cultures. Teachers in Taipei used these teaching techniques more frequently than teachers in Sendai, who in turn used them more frequently than the American teachers. Also, every child in Sendai and every classroom in Taipei is equipped with a mathematics "set"—a collection of colorful, interesting materials that are used extensively in illustrating and representing mathematics. Deprived of such frequent concrete experience with mathematics operations and concepts, American children are less able to solve problems involving the application of mathematics to situations outside the classroom. This does not mean that American children have mastered mathematics as an abstract representational system. For example, they were less able to explain the meaning of such symbols as the plus sign or to express a clear understanding of the significance of the equal sign.

The similarities between the Chinese and Japanese children's performance were greater than the differences in all but one respect. Chinese teachers emphasize the importance of speed in the solution of problems; Japanese teachers emphasize the importance of thoughtful consideration. The implications of this difference in approach are not clear at the elementary school level where both groups of children perform well. Long-term effects of the rapid-fire versus the more contemplative approach to mathematics may become evident during the later years of school.

We conclude from this study that curricular reform of elementary school mathematics in the United States cannot be limited to any specific domain. American children, far from being children who approach mathematics in novel, creative ways, are deficient in their understanding of the number system, in computation, in applying mathematical operations, and in relating mathematics to the real world. A large percentage of American children lack the understanding of the fundamental aspects of mathematics that make creative use of mathematics possible. Their deficiencies are so pervasive that teachers of secondary school mathematics cannot be expected to remedy the deficiencies and still have time to teach the new material needed for advances in knowledge. The results of this study suggest that American elementary school children have not been provided with the background of skills and knowledge that make it possible to benefit fully from the content of secondary school mathematics.

REFERENCES

Carpenter, Thomas P., and James M. Moser. "The Acquisition of Addition and Subtraction Concepts." In *Acquisition of Mathematics Concepts and Processes*, edited by Richard Lesh and Marsha Landau, pp. 7–24. New York: Academic Press, 1983.

Freedman, David, Robert Pisani, and Roger Purves. *Statistics*. New York: W. W. Norton & Co., 1980.

Fuson, Karen C., James W. Stigler, and Karen Bartsch. "Grade Placement of Addition and Subtraction Topics in Mainland China, Japan, the Soviet Union, Taiwan, and the United States." *Journal for Research in Mathematics Education* 19 (November 1988): 449–56.

Husén, Torsten. *International Study of Achievement in Mathematics*. New York: John Wiley & Sons, 1967.

McKnight, Curtis C., F. Joe Crosswhite, John A. Dossey, E. Kifer, Jane O. Swafford, Kenneth J. Travers, and Thomas J. Cooney. *The Underachieving Curriculum: Assessing U.S. School Mathematics from an International Perspective*. Champaign, Ill.: Stipes Publishing Co., 1987.

Riley, Mary S., James G. Greeno, and J. Heller. "Development of Children's Problem-solving Ability in Arithmetic." In *The Development of Mathematical Thinking*, edited by Herbert Ginsburg, pp. 153–96. New York: Academic Press, 1983.

Song, Myong J., and Herbert P. Ginsburg. "The Development of Informal and Formal Mathematical Thinking in Korean and U.S. Children." *Child Development* 58 (1987): 1286–96.

Stevenson, Harold W., Shin-Ying Lee, and James W. Stigler. "Mathematics Achievement of Chinese, Japanese, and American Children." *Science* 231 (1986): 693–99.

Stevenson, Harold W., Max Lummis, Shin-Ying Lee, and James W. Stigler. *Making the Grade in Mathematics: Elementary School Mathematics in the United States, Taiwan, and Japan.* Reston, Va.: National Council of Teachers of Mathematics, 1990.

Stevenson, Harold W., Shin-Ying Lee, Chuansheng Chen, James W. Stigler, Chen-chin Hsu, and Seiro Kitamura. *Contexts of Achievement: A Study of American, Chinese, and Japanese Children.* Monograph of the Society for Research in Child Development. Chicago: University of Chicago Press, in press.

Stigler, James W., Karen C. Fuson, Mark Ham, and Myong S. Kim. "An Analysis of Addition and Subtraction Word Problems in American and Soviet Elementary Mathematics Textbooks." *Cognition and Instruction* 3(3) (1986): 153–71.

Stigler, James W., Shin-Ying Lee, G. William Lucker, and Harold W. Stevenson. "Curriculum and Achievement in Mathematics: A Study of Elementary School Children in Japan, Taiwan, and the United States." *Journal of Educational Psychology* 74 (1982): 315–22.

Stigler, James W., and Michelle Perry. "Mathematics Learning in Japanese, Chinese, and American Classrooms." In *Children's Mathematics*, edited by Geoffrey Saxe and Mary L. Gearhart. San Francisco: Jossey-Bass, 1988.

Appendix A: Computation Test

First-graders started at item 1, fifth-graders at item 26. The first 15 questions were read aloud to first-graders, after which they worked independently. Fifth-graders worked independently on the test. For first 15 items, first-graders were told, "Everyone will please listen carefully. I will read the problems and you will write the answer in the box. Now let's start."

Numbers in this column represent percentage of children in Sendai, Taipei, and Chicago (in that order) who scored the item correct. Items 1 to 25 were given only to first grade children.

1. "Let's look at the first problem. How many dots are there? Write the answer in the box."

100, 99, 98

2. "What is the number that comes after 6? Write that number in the box."

99, 75, 90

3. "Next you see 5 plus 1. Write the answer in the box."

98, 96, 87

$$5 + 1 = \boxed{}$$

4. "Here you see five birds and four sets of bird-cages. Which set of bird-cages has one bird-cage for each bird? Circle that set of bird-cages."

98, 91, 84

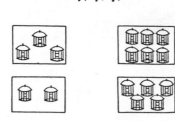

5. "Now look at the apple trees. Which tree has more apples? Circle that tree."   *100, 99, 99*

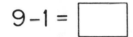

6. "Next you see 9 minus 1."   *80, 74, 52*

$$9 - 1 = \boxed{}$$

7. "How many dots are there?"   *100, 99, 99*

• • • •

$\boxed{}$

8. "Look at the next one. How many dots are there? Count them and write the answer in the box."   *96, 96, 78*

• • • • • • • • • • • • • • • •

$\boxed{}$

9. "Which basket has more eggs? Circle that basket."   *100, 99, 100*

10. "Look at the next one. Which number is bigger? Circle that number."   *100, 98, 95*

11. "Next you see 5 plus 4. Write the answer in the box."

$$5 + 4 = \boxed{}$$

99, 96, 77

12. "Next you see 8 minus 3. Write the answer in the box."

$$8 - 3 = \boxed{}$$

87, 71, 45

13. "The next problem is 6 minus 0. Write the answer in the box."

$$6 - 0 = \boxed{}$$

91, 77, 83

14. "The next problem is 17 minus 4. Write the answer in the box."

$$17 - 4 = \boxed{}$$

64, 53, 24

15. "Look at the next problem. Seventy-three, seventy-four . . . what comes next? Write the answer in the box." Wait until the child finishes writing '75,' go on and say, "And then what comes next? Write the answer in the box."

73, 74, ☐, ☐, 77, 78, 79, ☐, 81, 82

80, 71, 41

16. $14 + 5 = \boxed{}$ *78, 68, 35*

17. $19 + 25 = \boxed{}$ *18, 20, 7*

18. $14 - 6 = \boxed{}$ *35, 32, 15*

19.   **100, 200, 300, ☐, 500, 600, ☐, 800**   *83, 72, 59*

20.
$$\begin{array}{r} 62 \\ -36 \\ \hline \end{array}$$
2, 5, 1

21.
$$\begin{array}{r} 3 \\ 4 \\ +7 \\ \hline \end{array}$$
12, 23, 15

22. $662 \square 583$ *3, 3, 4*
     $(>, <)$

23. 37   *1, 2, 0*
     78
     +59

24. 123   *4, 10, 3*
     +453

25. 317   *1, 2, 0*
     −48

     Starting here, format is
     first-grade; fifth-grade

26. $5 \times 9 = \boxed{}$ *4, 14, 1;*
                                            98, 99, 96

27. $\boxed{} - 34 = 32$ *0, 2, 0;*
                                         87, 84, 29

28. 704   *0, 1, 0;*
     −268   *81, 89, 69*

29. $13 \div 13 = \boxed{}$ *0, 1, 0;*
                                            91, 93, 70

30. $14 \div 1 = \boxed{}$ *1, 1, 1;*
                                           96, 98, 81

31. $8 \times 0 = \boxed{}$ *1, 3, 2;*
                                            90, 75, 96

32. $712 \div 89 = 8$ *0, 0, 0;*
                          87, 91, 68
     $8 \times 89 = \boxed{}$

33. $42 \div 6 = \boxed{}$ *1, 1, 1;*
                                           95, 96, 81

34.
$$\begin{array}{r} 198 \\ \times\ 4 \\ \hline \end{array}$$

0, 0, 0;
93, 94, 73

35.
$$\begin{array}{r} 206 \\ \times\ 3 \\ \hline \end{array}$$

0, 0, 0;
97, 97, 73

36. **3457 = (3 × 1000) + (4 × 100) + (5 × 10) + 7**

2683 = [   ]

0, 0, 0;
73, 82, 45

37.
$$6\overline{)432}$$

0, 0, 0;
94, 94, 53

38.
$$5\overline{)3281}$$

0, 0, 0;
86, 90, 49

39.

$$\frac{1}{3}$$ $$\frac{1}{\boxed{\ }}$$

2, 11, 6;
97, 99, 89

40.
$$6\overline{)1586}$$

0, 0, 0;
94, 96, 48

41.   **98634 □ 98745
(<, >)**

0, 1, 1;
95, 96, 77

First-grade test went only to this point; rest of percentages are for fifth grade only.

42.
$$\begin{array}{r} 45 \\ \times 26 \\ \hline \end{array}$$

90, 90, 54

43. $5.3 - 4.6 = \boxed{}$ *81, 87, 41*

44. $46\overline{)3572}$ *67, 80, 15*

45. $\dfrac{3}{8} + \dfrac{2}{8} = \boxed{}$ *95, 90, 39*

46. $\begin{array}{r} 38.15 \\ -\ 9.43 \\ \hline \end{array}$ *73, 83, 54*

47. $3600\overline{)843000}$ *30, 54, 5*

48. $\begin{array}{r} 353 \\ \times\ 477 \\ \hline \end{array}$ *66, 65, 25*

49. $2\dfrac{3}{5} \ \square \ \dfrac{4}{5}$
        $(<, >)$ *93, 94, 69*

50. $\dfrac{5}{7} - \dfrac{2}{7} = \boxed{}$ *92, 96, 41*

51. $12\overline{)13.08}$ *58, 81, 49*

52. $2.079 \ \square \ 2.465$
        $(<, >)$ *92, 94, 66*

53. $\begin{array}{r} 0.034 \\ \times\ \ \ 17 \\ \hline \end{array}$ *63, 64, 16*

54.
$$\frac{1}{2} = \frac{\square}{6}$$
62, 87, 31

55.
$$\begin{array}{r} 46.725 \\ -\ 23.123 \\ \hline \end{array}$$
80, 85, 63

56.
$$2\frac{4}{6} + \frac{3}{6} = \boxed{}$$
82, 89, 25

57.
$$.025\overline{)36}$$
9, 3, 0

58.
$$\frac{3}{4} - \frac{1}{6} = \boxed{\ -\ }$$
7, 11, 1

59.
$$0.08 \times 10 = \boxed{}$$
67, 72, 21

60.
$$\frac{3}{8} \div 4 = \boxed{}$$
4, 1, 0

61.
$$\frac{1}{5} \ \square \ \frac{1}{6}$$
$(<, >)$
55, 50, 23

62.
$$\frac{1}{4} = \boxed{0.}$$
7, 9, 1

63.
$$2\frac{3}{4} \times \frac{1}{6} = \boxed{}$$
6, 1, 0

64.
$$\frac{8}{9} \times 4 = \boxed{}$$
14, 9, 1

65. $\dfrac{3}{5} \times \dfrac{1}{9} =$ [   ] *25, 33, 26*

66. $0.02 = \dfrac{2}{\square}$ *30, 14, 2*

67. $6 \times \dfrac{4}{7} =$ [   ] *13, 7, 2*

68. $\dfrac{1}{3} =$ [0.   ] *3, 2, 2*

69. $1\dfrac{2}{3} \div \dfrac{7}{8} =$ [   ] *5, 0, 0*

70. $\dfrac{5}{11} \div \dfrac{1}{9} =$ [   ] *5, 1, 0*

71. $12 \div \dfrac{8}{9} =$ [   ] *4, 1, 0*

72. $3 : 10 =$ [   ] $: 100$ *11, 17, 3*

73. $4\dfrac{1}{7} \div 2 =$ [   ] *5, 1, 0*

74. $0.33 \times \dfrac{1}{3} =$ [   ] *5, 2, 0*

75. $5 + (-4) =$ [   ] *20, 25, 24*

Appendix B: Individual Tests

The materials for the Mathematics Assessment Battery consisted of three parts; a test booklet, the examiner's instructions, and a worksheet for recording the student's responses. The test was given on two consecutive days. The tests for Day 1 were word problems, operations, visualization, and graphing. On Day 2 the remaining tests were given: oral problems, mental calculation, number concepts and equations, estimation, and mental folding. The tests were given to the students in the orders listed. The geometry test is included here but was administered as a group test.

The majority of the tests were the same for both first and fifth grades. It is noted where the tests or certain problems differed for each grade.

In this description of the tests, the examiner's instructions to the student are in quotes. The problems and pictures in the test booklet are in boldface type. In the margin to the right of most of the problems the percentage of students in each city who answered the problem correctly is included. Typically, the first three percentages are for the first grade students and the second three are for the fifth grade students. The three scores at each grade follow the order: Sendai, Taipei, Chicago.

Contents

The numbers appearing in this column report the percentage of children in each city and grade who answered the adjacent item correctly. When two lines of numbers are presented, the first line is always first grade, the second line fifth grade. Within each line, the order always is Sendai, Taipei, Chicago.

I. Word Problems

A. Instructions

Materials. Booklet with one problem on each page to be shown to child. Pencils and paper.

Practice problem 1. E (Examiner) says:

> Now we are going to do some word problems. In these word problems I'll read you the problem and then you tell me the answer.

E displays the card to S as E reads the problem. Let's try one together.

E reads the practice problem: Sam had 2 toys
and got 1 more toy. How many toys did Sam
have altogether?

If the child cannot answer the question E says:

> If Sam had 2 toys and got one more toy,
> then he would have 3 toys, wouldn't he?
> Two toys and one toy are three toys
> altogether. Now let's go to the next
> problem.

E offers S some paper and a pencil and says:

> You can use these if you want to. I'll
> read each problem once, but I'll be glad
> to read it again if you ask me to.

Criterion for stopping. All children, both first
and fifth graders, start with problem 1. E stops
the test if S misses 2 problems for each of 2
consecutive semesters. For example, E would
stop the test if S misses the problems for grade
1-2 and the two problems for grade 2-1.

E then says,

> Let's look at a few more problems. I'll
> read the problem to you and you tell me
> if you would like to try it.

If the child either does not try the next two
problems or misses two more successive
problems, the test is stopped.

The E allows a maximum of 90 sec for each
problem. If the child appears not to understand
what should be done and fails to make any
efforts at calculation, E suggests:

> Is this one too hard? Shall we go to the
> next one?

If the child is working on the problem but has not completed it after 90 sec, E says:

> You are doing fine on that one. You don't have to finish it for me. Let's go to the next one.

B. Problems

1 (K–1)	Joey had 3 marbles and then found 2 more. How many marbles does Joey have now?	98, 97, 89; 100, 99, 100
2 (K–2)	Jan's father gave her 6 cookies. She ate 2 of them. How many did she have left?	93, 81, 73; 99, 100, 97
3 (1–1)	Some squirrels picked up 9 nuts yesterday and 4 nuts today. How many nuts do they have altogether?	88, 76, 64; 100, 98, 98
4 (1–1)	There were 15 bunnies. 9 hopped away. How many bunnies were left?	66, 38, 30; 96, 98, 88
5 (1–2)	Lisa invited 4 friends to a party. Then she invited 3 more friends. But 2 friends could not come. How many of Lisa's friends came to the party?	68, 50, 42; 96, 92, 86
6 (1–2)	Let's say that you had 6 jellybeans and your friend has 4 and you both want to have the same number of jellybeans. How many of your jellybeans would you have to give your friend so that both of you would have the same number?	58, 44, 17; 93, 86, 71
7 (2–1)	Chris has 26 toy cars. Mary has 19. How many do they have in all?	29, 25, 13; 96, 96, 86

8 (2–1)   **One day there were some apples**   *21, 13, 3;*
            under a tree. The next day 6 more   *94, 88, 69*
            apples fell to the ground. Now there
            are 14 apples on the ground. How
            many apples were on the ground on
            the first day?

9 (2–2)   **Marty measured a tree and it was**   *6, 2, 1;*
            139 inches tall. A few months later it *89, 80, 59*
            was 168 inches tall. How much had it
            grown since Marty measured it the
            first time?

10 (2–2)   **There were 3 boxes. Each box had 4**   *52, 34, 11;*
            books in it. How many books were   *99, 98, 85*
            there in all?

11 (3–1)   **Kim's weight is 49.7 pounds. Sue's**
            weight is 50.4 pounds.

            (a) Who is heavier?   *49, 40, 16;*
                                                        100, 100, 94

            (b) How much heavier?   *0, 0, 0;*
                                                        74, 70, 26

12 (3–1)   **8 children went on a picnic. Each**   *8, 8, 4;*
            child took 2 sandwiches and 3   *96, 85, 75*
            cookies. Altogether, how many
            cookies did the children take?

13 (3–2)   **The teacher gave 3 sheets of paper**   *5, 4, 1;*
            to each of 9 people. There are still 2 *88, 90, 43*
            sheets of paper left. How many
            sheets of paper did the teacher have
            when he began?

14 (3–2)   **33 people went to a football game.**   *8, 4, 2;*
            They went home in 7 cars. In 6 of   *92, 82, 54*
            the cars, there were 5 people each.
            How many people were in the
            seventh car?

15 (4–1) **Dad cut a cake into 16 pieces. George ate one fourth of them. How many pieces were left?**   *1, 1, 2; 65, 63, 30*

16 (4–1) **A field was 20 meters long and 15 wide. How long is the fence that goes completely around the field?**   *3, 0, 0; 42, 18, 15*

17 (4–2) **A stamp collecting club has 24 members. Five-sixths of the members collect only foreign stamps. How many members collect only foreign stamps?**   *2, 0, 0; 43, 35, 9*

18 (4–2) **John is saving his money to buy a baseball bat that costs $20.00. For the first 4 months, he will be able to save $2.00 a month. Each month after that he will be able to save $3.00 a month. How many months will it take to save enough money to buy the bat?**   *1, 2, 0; 54, 35, 26*

19 (5–1) **An apple has 0.4 grams of protein and an orange has 1.5 grams of protein. A girl ate 3 apples and 2 oranges. How many grams of protein did she eat?**   *0, 0, 0; 68, 63, 17*

20 (5–1) **A truck will hold only 33 boxes of oranges. How many trips will be needed to carry 152 boxes of oranges to a store?**   *1, 0, 1; 52, 54, 15*

21 (5–2) **A train left Chicago at 1:55 p.m. and arrived at St. Louis 6 hours and 52 minutes later. What time did the train arrive in St. Louis?**   *0, 0, 0; 34, 27, 3*

22 (5–2) **A farmer has a square tank that needs to be filled with water. The tank holds 125 cubic feet of water.**   *5th: 8, 0, 2*

As the farmer fills the tank, the level of the water rises at the rate of 1 foot per hour. How many cubic feet of water will be in the tank after 1 hour?

23 (6–1)   A bookstore had 1,100 books. Last week, 15% of the books were sold. How many books are left?

5th: 8, 8, 1

24 (6–1)   Diane dropped a special rubber ball from the top of a wall. The wall is 16 feet high. Each time the ball hits the ground it bounces up half as high as the distance it fell. Diane caught the ball when it bounced back to a high point of 1 foot. How many times did the ball hit the ground?

5th: 40, 18, 6

25 (6–2)   A 42-year-old father has a 9-year-old son. In how many years will the son's age be one quarter of the father's age?

5th: 14, 3, 2

26 (6–2)   A plumber knows that it takes 12 minutes to saw a piece of copper pipe into 3 pieces. How long would it take to saw it into 4 pieces?

5th: 5, 0, 0

27 (7–1)   A lake resort owner rented a cabin for 14 days on the condition that she would receive 40 dollars a day for every day it did not rain and 10 dollars a day for every day it did rain. At the end of 2 weeks, the resort owner received 380 dollars. How many days did it rain?

5th: 9, 2, 1

II. Oral Test (First Grade Only)

A. Instructions

1. For this test, E should record the time it takes the child to finish all the questions.
2. If the child says "I don't know" or if 30 seconds have passed without the child answering, go on to the next question. E says, "That's OK. Let's do another one."
3. Read all the questions in this test to the child.

B. Problems

"I am going to read you some problems. You tell me the answer. I will read the problem again if you want me to. If the problem is too hard, we will go on to some other questions."

1. "There were 3 apples and 2 pears on a plate. The children ate all the fruit for lunch. How many pears were left on the plate?"   *83, 83, 67*

2. "Kate is 3 years older than her brother. How many years older than her brother will Kate be in 5 years?"   *23, 16, 6*

3. "A teacher has to correct 30 notebooks. All the notebooks but three have been corrected. How many notebooks does the teacher still have to correct?"   *44, 28, 27*

4. "Alesha told her mother that she met Carol 3 times today, and Carol told her mother that she met Alesha 3 times. How many times did Alesha and Carol meet each other today?"   *46, 26, 44*

5. "I have 50 envelopes and 60 sheets of paper.   *46, 44, 19*
   What is the largest number of letters that I
   can mail?"

6. "2 boys and 2 girls picked strawberries. One   *94, 83, 81*
   girl picked the most of all and one boy picked
   the least of all. Did the girls pick more
   strawberries than the boys?"

III. Number Concepts and Equations

A. Instructions

Give the child the answer sheet and a pencil.
(The answer sheet will be used for questions 1
and 5.) For this part of the test, all children
should do questions 1 to 9. Starting from
question 10, if the child answers incorrectly or
says "I don't know" for 5 successive questions,
then E asks "Do you want to try another?" If
yes, present the problem, let the child try it,
and ask them if they want to try the next one.
Continue the same process until the child
says"No". Then go on to the Estimation Test.

B. Problems

1. First Grade

                                                         First Grade

1. a. "Write the number three." (Present the   *100, 99, 95*
      answer sheet.)

   b. "Write the number seventeen."   *99, 98, 92*

   c. "Write the number fifty-seven."   *96, 98, 92*

   d. "Please write the number that is ten more   *50, 28, 31*
      than fifty-seven."

2. "Can you count for me how many dots are here?" Have the child count 17 dots. Ask the child:

   a. "How much further can you count? Please count for me." (Stop the child at 32.) *94, 97, 96*

   b. Then say, "Pretend you have counted to 67. Now start counting at 68 and go on." (Stop at 72.) *96, 94, 81*

   c. Then say, "Pretend you have counted to 97. Now start at 97." (Stop at 102.) *83, 63, 80*

3. "Which of these numbers shows one hundred thirty-two?" *70, 38, 25*

10032 **132** **32**

4. "Which of the following is the largest number?"

   a. **12** **102** **120** **21** *91, 87, 76*

   b. **502** **5000** **520** **900** *92, 73, 74*

5. "Draw a circle around one-half the stars." (On the answer sheet) *52, 30, 11*

☆☆☆ ☆☆☆ ☆

☆ ☆ ☆ ☆☆

6. "Which figure is divided into four equal parts?" *83, 88, 88*

   a. .b. c. d.

7. "There are many ways to say 5. You could say   *93, 88, 81*
   3 + 2, 1 + 1 + 3, 6 − 1, etc. Tell me all the
   ways you could use numbers to come up with
   the number 6." (Allow maximum of 30
   seconds.)

8. "What sign should replace the square in   *87, 69, 61*
   6 ☐ 3 = 3"
   +   −   ×   ÷   =

9. "John had six marbles. He gave two marbles   *92, 58, 80*
   to Sam. Now he has four left. Which of these
   number sentences best shows this?"

   a. 6 − 2 = 4

   b. 6 − 4 = 2

   c. 4 − 2 = 2

10. Here is a picture. Can you tell me which   *90, 63, 69*
    equation goes with this picture?

    a. 5 − 2 = 3

    b. 6 − 3 = 3

    c. 7 − 4 = 3

11. "Can you figure out the number that fits in
    the blank?" (Each equation on a separate
    page.)

    a. **4 + 6 = _____ + 4**   *30, 9, 15*

    b. **4 + 6 + 3 = _____ + 3**   *17, 8, 3*

    c. **10 + _____ = 10**   *59, 31, 34*

12. "What is the number before 2?" (There are no pictures on the next three problems.) *81, 42, 74*

13. "What is the number before 1?" *82, 48, 71*

14. "Can you read this for me?" (Each on its own page.)
    a. **498**   b. **30%**   c. **800070**

    (a) 69, 32, 47
    (b) 34, 1, 17
    (c) 8, 1, 3

15. "Here is a number sentence: **10 − __ − __ = 6.** One of the numbers **0,2,3,5** can fit in both squares. Which number is this?" *52, 18, 15*

16. "Can you make up a number expression that uses:" **4 ☐ 1 ☐ 3**
    +   −   ×   ÷   =

    68, 29, 24

17. "What is the number that is the same as ten tens?" *17, 30, 10*

18. a. "Here are 3 digits, **3, 6, 1.** How could you arrange these three digits to form the biggest number?" *40, 28, 28*

    b. "How could you arrange these three digits to form the smallest number?" *40, 28, 27*

19. "What is the number before 0?" *8, 0, 1*

(If the child gets question 19 wrong ask question 20.)

20. "Do you think it is possible to have a number before 0?" *18, 6, 4*

2. Fifth Grade

(Answer sheet is used for questions 2, 10, and 11) *Fifth Grade*

1. "Which of these numbers shows one hundred thirty-two?" *100, 100, 92*
   10032   **132**   **32**

2. "Draw a circle around one-half the stars."   *97, 83, 71*
   (on the answer sheet)

☆☆☆   ☆☆☆   ☆

☆   ☆   ☆   ☆☆

3. "What sign should replace the square in   *98, 99, 98*
   6 ☐ 3 = 18"
   +   **×**   **−**   **÷**   **=**

4. "What signs would you place between the   *89, 78, 76*
   numbers to complete this problem?"

   5 __ 3 __ 2

5. "What sign goes in this box to make this   *92, 86, 64*
   number sentence true?"

   5 ☐ 4 = 3 × 3

6. "Which equation best represents the   *63, 45, 44*
   picture below?"

   a. **3 + 4 = 7**
   b. **12 + 3 + 3 = 18**
   c. **12 ÷ 4 = 3**
   d. **(3 × 5) − 3 = 12**

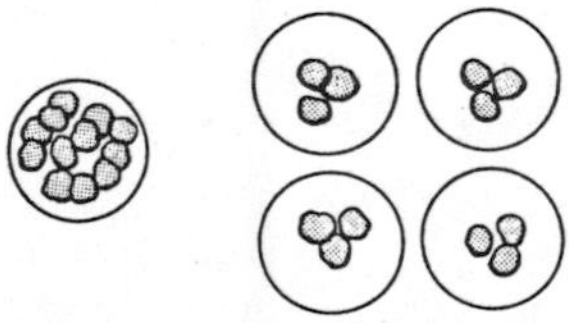

7. "There are many ways to say 5. You could say   *98, 100, 94*
   3 + 2, 1 + 1 + 3, 6 − 1, etc. Tell me all the
   ways you could use numbers to come up with
   the number 6." (Allow maximum of 30
   seconds.) *Percentage refers to subjects giving
   any valid response.*

8. "Solve these problems." (Each on its own page.)

    a. $4 + 6 + 3 = \underline{\hphantom{xx}} + 3$ *90, 85, 39*

    b. $(4 + 5) + 2 = 4 + \underline{\hphantom{xx}}$ *88, 90, 42*

    c. $8 \times 7 = 7 \times \underline{\hphantom{xx}}$ *97, 99, 71*

    d. $9 \times \underline{\hphantom{xx}} = 0$ *97, 98, 100*

9. "Can you read this for me?"   (Each on its own page.)

    a. **498**   b. **30%**   c. **800070**   d. **20350076**

a. 100, 97, 98
b. 100, 81, 92
c. 96, 90, 53
d. 96, 76, 45

10. (Show problem and read to child.) "Try to write an equation (on answer sheet) by which you could solve this problem." **"The school needs 100 flags for a holiday celebration. A number of flags were produced on the first day and another 21 remained to be made. How many flags were produced on the first day?"**

94, 97, 60

11. "How would you write the number three-fourths?" (Present the answer sheet.)

100, 95, 93

12. "Can you tell me what portion of the clock lies in the shaded region between the two hands?"

77, 68, 27

13. "Name the numeral in the tens place for:"
    (Each on its own page.)

    a. **52043**   *100, 98, 83*

    b. **89**   *100, 99, 88*

    c. **1057**   *100, 99, 90*

14. "Can you tell me another way to say 1/2?"   *94, 75, 40*

15. "What is the number before 1?"   *88, 73, 96*

16. a. "What is the number before 0?"   *25, 5, 11*

    b. If the child gets 16a. wrong, ask "Do you   *56, 50, 12*
       think it is possible to have a number less
       than 0?"

17. "Is -3 greater or lesser than -2?"   *68, 62, 31*

18. "What sign goes in this box to make this   *84, 68, 42*
    number sentence true?"

                 100 ☐ 5 > 150 − 5

    +   **×**   **−**   **÷**   **>**

19. "Which of these is a way to find one-half of   *73, 61, 44*
    six?"

    6 ÷ 2   6 ÷ 1/2   6 − 2   6 × 1/2   6 + 1/2

20. "Put parentheses to show how this problem
    was solved. Here is an example:

        8 + (7 + 4) = 8 + 11"

    a. **5 + 4 − 3 = 5 + 1**   *88, 72, 62*

    b. **48 = 4 × 2 + 4 × 2**   *64, 53, 30*

21. "Ten cans of pop cost $1.50 at one store. I   *83, 67, 38*
    can get 5 cans for 80 cents at a second store.
    Where is the pop cheaper? The first or the
    second store?

22. "John had 6 apples. He cut each of the   *50, 61, 31*
    apples into 4 pieces. He gave an equal
    number of pieces to each of 3 friends. Pick
    the equation that you can use to figure out
    how many pieces each friend got."

    a. $(6 \times 4) \div 3 =$

    b. $(6 \div 4) \times 3 =$

    c. $3 \times (6 \times 1/4) =$

23. a. "Here are 5 digits, **2, 6, 3, 5, 1**. How   *91, 76, 59*
    could you arrange these digits to form the
    biggest number?"

    b. "How could you arrange these digits to   *93, 77, 57*
    form the smallest number?" **2, 6, 3, 5, 1**

24. "Solve **8 − 12 = ?**"   *33, 28, 5*

IV. Estimation

A. *Instructions*

1. For this test, E should record the time it
   takes the child to finish all the questions.
2. Allow only 10 seconds for each response. If
   child doesn't answer in this time, E says,
   "Let's go on to the next problem, OK?"
3. Present all the questions in this test to the
   child.

"Now I am going to ask you some questions and
I want you to tell me the best answer you can
think of. Just tell me what you think the best
answer is."

B. Problems

1. First Grade and Fifth Grade

Items 1 and 2 scored correct if answer correct plus or minus 1.

1. "About how many paper clips lined up in a row would be as long as this pencil?"

   75, 61, 51;
   93, 93, 89

2. a. "If each yard on this map is this long (point), how many yards is it from the tree to the treasure?"

   25, 8, 20;
   38, 28, 26

   b. "About how far is it from the tree to the footprints?"

   20, 6, 21;
   38, 23, 18

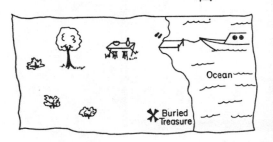

3. a. "There are 3 lines here. Can you tell me which line shows 2 inches?"

   51, 39, 31;
   69, 73, 44

   b. "Which line shows 4 inches?"

   55, 23, 63;
   76, 63, 74

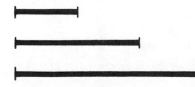

Items 4 a–d scored correct if answer within 10% of total numerical length of line.

4. a. "Look at this line. This is 1 and this is 100. What number do you think X is?"

11, 10, 4;
80, 76, 45

b. "Here is another line. This is 0 and this is 10. What number do you think X is?"

70, 44, 26;
96, 96, 87

c. "This is 80 and this is 100. What number do you think X is?"

66, 34, 40;
94, 81, 68

d. "One more line. This is 500 and this is 700. What number do you think X is?"

6, 5, 3;
90, 73, 41

First Grade

5. a. "Look at the dots. Can you tell me how many dots you think are on this page? Would you say there are 20, 40, 60, or 80 dots?" (Present the card for only 3 seconds.)

43, 18, 12

b. "How about this one? Would you say there   *29, 10, 10*
are 45, 65, 85, or 105 dots?" (Present the
card for only 3 seconds.)

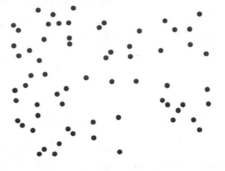

2. *Fifth Grade Only*

The fifth grade test was identical to the first
grade test up to this point, except that the order
in which the items 1 through 5 were presented
was 1, 2, 5, 3, and 7. On item 7, the dot
configurations for fifth grade differed from
those presented to first graders, and so that
item is reproduced here. In addition, the
following two questions appeared as items 4 and
6 on the fifth grade test.

Fifth Grade

7. a. "There are some dots here. Look at the   *46, 38, 31*
dots. Can you tell me how many dots you
think are on this page? Would you say there
are 45, 95, 125, or 155 dots?" (Present the
card for only 3 seconds.)

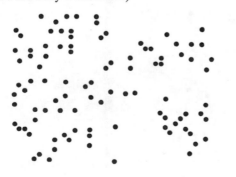

b. "How about this one? Would you say there are 120, 160, 200, or 240 dots?" (Present the card for only 3 seconds.) *35, 22, 32*

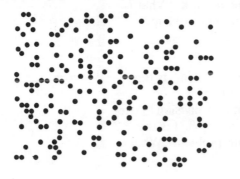

4. "If the small block of ice weighs two lbs., about how much does the larger block weigh?" *18, 5, 8*

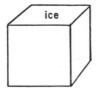

6. "Which two numbers multiplied together would give an answer closest to the target number?"

a.	2	18	50	37	**75**	*68, 68, 47*
b.	26	16	41	5	**1000**	*53, 58, 56*

V. Operations

A. First Grade

The E says, "Now let's do something different." (Child sees problem in boldface type.)

For next 4 problems, percentages are for first part of question (i.e., identifying the operation)

1. **6 − 2**   "Look at this problem. Is this   *99, 98, 84*
                addition, subtraction,
                multiplication, or division?"
                After S responds, ask "What is
                the answer to this problem?
                What is 6 − 2?"

2. **3 + 4**   "Look at this problem. Is this   *100, 95, 65*
                addition, subtraction,
                multiplication, or division? After
                S responds, ask "What is the
                answer to this problem? What is
                3 + 4?"

3. **8 ÷ 2**   "Look at this problem. Is this   *63, 36, 39*
                addition, subtraction,
                multiplication, or division?"
                After S responds, ask "What is
                the answer to this problem?
                What is 8 ÷ 2?"

4. **3 × 5**   "Look at this problem. Is this   *77, 37, 39*
                addition, subtraction,
                multiplication, or division?"
                After S responds, ask "What is
                the answer to this problem? What
                is 3 × 5?"

5. **5 + 2 = ?**   "I was asking you some word
                problems a few minutes ago. Now
                here are some numbers. Suppose
                you are a teacher and you want to
                make up some questions. What
                kind of word problem would you
                make up using these numbers?"

Allow 1 minute for response. Record child's
answer as accurately as possible. After one
minute, say, "That's fine. Let's go on." If child
doesn't answer or says, "don't know," go on to
the next question. (The following three problems
use this format for the child's response.)

6. **8 − 6 = ?** "Here is another one. Can you make up a word problem for me using these numbers?"

7. "Pretend that some Martians came to visit you and they had never heard of addition. If they asked you to tell them all the ways you could use addition, what would you tell them?"

8. "The Martians also had never heard of subtraction. They asked you to tell them all the ways to use subtraction. What would you tell them?"

B. Fifth Grade

E says, "Now let's do something different. Can you tell me . . ." (Child sees problem in boldface type.)

1. a) What is **5 + 7**?   *100, 100, 97*
   b) What is **50 + 70**?   *100, 99, 91*
   c) What is **500 + 700**?   *99, 96, 89*
   d) What is **500 + 70**?   *99, 98, 87*

2. a) What is **3 × 6**?   *100, 100, 98*
   b) What is **30 × 60**?   *73, 74, 35*
   c) What is **300 × 600**?   *73, 65, 13*

3. **4 × 3 = ?** "I was asking you some word problems a few minutes ago. Now here are some numbers. Suppose you are a teacher and you want to make up some questions. What kind of word problem would you make up using these numbers?"

Allow 1 minute for response. Record child's answer as accurately as possible. After one minute, say "That's fine. Let's go on." If child doesn't answer or says "don't know," go on to the next question.

4. **30 ÷ 6 = ?** "Here is another one. Can you make up a word problem for me using these numbers?"

Allow 1 minute for response. Record child's answer as accurately as possible. After one minute, say "That's fine. Let's go on." If child doesn't answer or says "don't know," go on to the next question.

5. "What are all the ways you can use multiplication of two whole numbers to come up with 24? (There is no written problem for child to see.)

6. Show **108 ÷ 24.** "Would you guess that the answer is less than 10 or more than 10?"

7. "Pretend that some Martians came to visit you and they had never heard of addition. If they asked you to tell them all the ways you could use addition, what would you tell them?"

Allow 1 minute for response. Record child's answer as accurately as possible. After one minute, say "That's fine. Let's go on." If child doesn't answer or says, "I don't know," go on to the next question.

8. "The Martians also had never heard of division. They asked you to tell them all the ways to use division. What would you tell them?"

Allow 1 minute for response. Record child's answer as accurately as possible. After one minute, say "That's fine. Let's go on." If child doesn't answer or says, "I don't know," go on to the next question.

VI. Geometry (Fifth Grade Only)

The geometry test, in contrast to the other tests in this appendix, was administered as a group test to fifth grade students immediately after they had completed the computation test. Students were allowed 20 minutes to work on the geometry test.

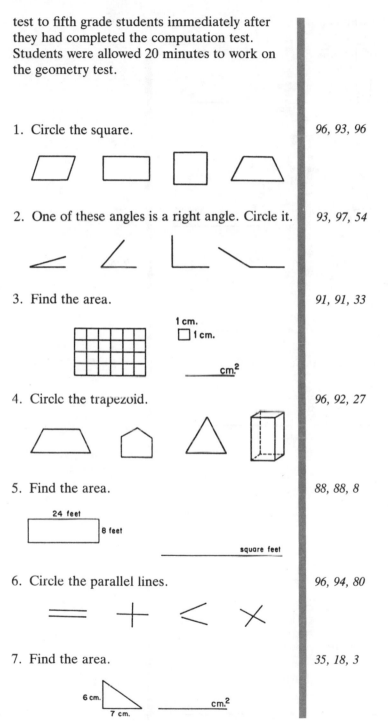

1. Circle the square.

96, 93, 96

2. One of these angles is a right angle. Circle it.

93, 97, 54

3. Find the area.

91, 91, 33

1 cm.
1 cm.

_____ cm.²

4. Circle the trapezoid.

96, 92, 27

5. Find the area.

88, 88, 8

24 feet
8 feet

_____ square feet

6. Circle the parallel lines.

96, 94, 80

7. Find the area.

35, 18, 3

6 cm.
7 cm.
_____ cm.²

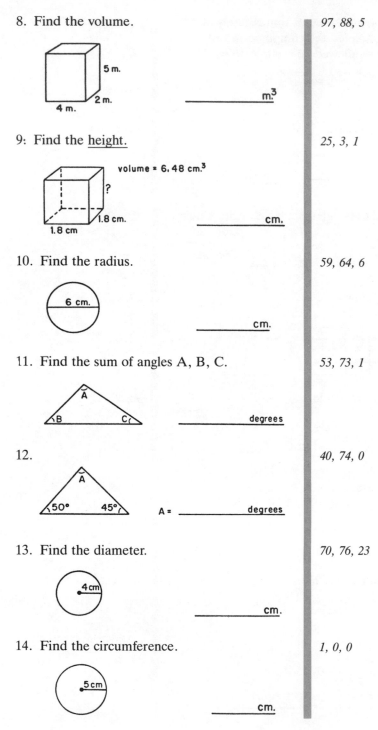

8. Find the volume.   *97, 88, 5*

5 m.

2 m.

4 m.

_____ m.³

9: Find the height.   *25, 3, 1*

volume = 6.48 cm.³

?

1.8 cm.

1.8 cm

_____ cm.

10. Find the radius.   *59, 64, 6*

6 cm.

_____ cm.

11. Find the sum of angles A, B, C.   *53, 73, 1*

A

B   C

_____ degrees

12.   *40, 74, 0*

A

50°   45°   A = _____ degrees

13. Find the diameter.   *70, 76, 23*

4 cm

_____ cm.

14. Find the circumference.   *1, 0, 0*

5 cm

_____ cm.

15. If the box were unfolded, which of these 3 pictures shows what it would look like? Circle that box.

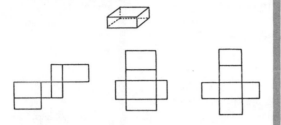

96, 93, 67

16,17. Match each equation with a line on the graph.

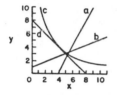

16. x + y = 8 _____

17. x × y = 16 _____

16. *38, 30, 15*
17. *21, 14, 8*

VII. Graphing

A. First Grade

1. "Let's look at something different." "Three children had puppies. This table tells us about the children and their puppies."

	Number of Black Puppies	Number of White Puppies
Sarah	4	1
Robert	2	4
Amy	3	0

(E reads table to child, but does not explain what it means.)

   a. "How many black puppies did Sarah have?"

79, 54, 55

b. "How many white puppies did Robert have?"   *81, 53, 44*

c. "Who had no white puppies?"   *96, 90, 81*

d. "Who had the most puppies?"   *84, 69, 42*

If the child misses all four of the preceding questions, skip the rest of the questions on the Graphing test.

2. "Now let's do something more difficult. If you don't understand it, that's OK. We will do something else."

   "Have you ever seen a bar graph? These are bar graphs. Each bar shows how many puppies each child has." (E points to each bar of the graph.) "First look at the table, then look at the graphs. Can you tell me which graph shows the number of puppies and their owners correctly?" (Allow 30 seconds for response.)   *40, 26, 23*

	Number of Black Puppies	Number of White Puppies
Sarah	4	1
Robert	2	4
Amy	3	0

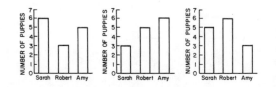

3. "Sarah weighed one of her puppies each month. This graph shows how her puppy grew."
   a. "How much did Sarah's puppy weigh in October?"   *58, 33, 40*

b. "How much did it weigh in December?"   *59, 27, 28*

c. "At what month did her puppy weigh the most?"   *42, 5, 4*

d. "At what month did her puppy weigh the least?"   *72, 33, 50*

4. "Here is another way to show who had more puppies. Look at the table about the puppies again. Which picture tells us correctly how many puppies Sarah, Robert, and Amy had?"

	Number of Black Puppies	Number of White Puppies
Sarah	4	1
Robert	2	4
Amy	3	0

B. Fifth Grade

E reads questions to the child, but the child only sees the graph.

1. "Here is a table with information about the members of a sports team."

   a. "How many members of the sports team are listed?"   *100, 84, 100*

   b. "Who is the shortest member?"   *98, 98, 98*

   c. "Find the average age of the first three members listed in the table."   *76, 75, 44*

   d. "How much heavier is the heaviest member of the team than the lightest member?"   *83, 82, 67*

Member	Age	Height	Weight	Favorite Event
Jack	9	52 inches	60 pounds	Running
Jill	11	57 inches	82 pounds	Jumping
Beth	10	55 inches	71 pounds	Jumping
Sally	11	56 inches	85 pounds	Jumping
Chris	12	57 inches	89 pounds	Swimming
Bob	12	60 inches	96 pounds	Running

If the child cannot answer any one of these 4 questions correctly, skip the rest of the questions on the graphing test and go on to the Motivation Test.

2. "Here is a bar graph of some of the information from the table. What do you think it shows?" Record child's response as accurately as possible.   *93, 78, 67*

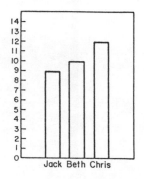

3. "Three members of the club had a race. The graph shows the result. Please look at the graph and tell me who won."

83, 58, 65

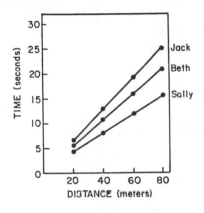

4. "Here is a blank circle graph that shows the sports team members' favorite events. Please tell me which event A should be. Running, jumping, or swimming?

99, 71, 80

Member	Age	Height	Weight	Favorite Event
Jack	9	52 inches	60 pounds	Running
Jill	11	57 inches	82 pounds	Jumping
Beth	10	55 inches	71 pounds	Jumping
Sally	11	56 inches	85 pounds	Jumping
Chris	12	57 inches	89 pounds	Swimming
Bob	12	60 inches	96 pounds	Running

Which event should be filled in B? Running, jumping, or swimming?

98, 77, 83

Which event should be filled in C? Running, jumping, or swimming?"

98, 84, 84

VIII. Visualization

A. *Instructions*

1. For this test, the time it takes the child to finish all the questions should be recorded.
2. If the child says she/he does not know or if 30 seconds have passed without the child answering, go on to the next question. E says, "This is OK. Let's do another one."
3. Read all the questions in this test to the child.

All the problems in this test were presented to both Grade 1 and Grade 5 children except where indicated.

B. *Problems*

1. "These are two rolled-up strings. Which of them is longer?"

97, 91, 67;
100, 100, 93

2. "Which puzzle piece will fit in the black part?"

88, 78, 77;
99, 85, 92

3. "Are these two parts the same shape?"

100, 92, 82;
98, 83, 88

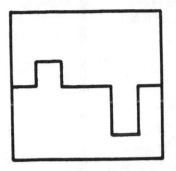

4. "Are these two parts the same shape?"

53, 37, 39;
82, 88, 81

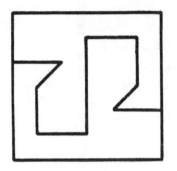

5. a. "If you pull the ends of this rope, would it or wouldn't it form a knot?"

(a)
93, 85, 78;
100, 99, 96

b. "How about this one? If you pull the ends of this rope, would it or wouldn't it form a knot?"

(b)
93, 93, 87;
99, 99, 98

c. "How about this one? If you pull the ends of this rope, would it or wouldn't it form a knot?"

(c)
83, 68, 61;
97, 95, 84

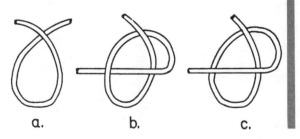

a.   b.   c.

6. "This is a ferris wheel with four people on it.
(Point out the people.) Who will be at the
highest point on the ferris wheel after it has
gone around 3 1/2 times?"

36, 26, 34;
83, 58, 52

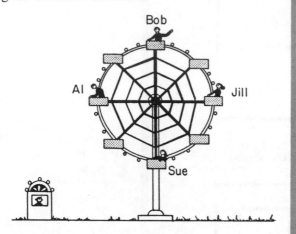

7. "On the left is a picture of a piece of paper
which has been folded and has a piece cut out at
the fold. The arrow points to the place where
the piece was cut out. How will the cutout piece
look when it is unfolded?"

79, 58, 39;
98, 96, 81

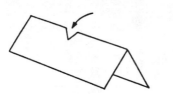

8. "What shape completes the square?"

In the problems 8–10,
students were not
allowed to rotate the
paper.

98, 97, 94;
100, 100, 98

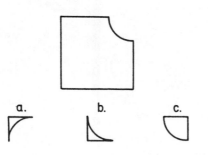

9. "What shape completes the square?"   *68, 53, 60;*
                                          92, 76, 77

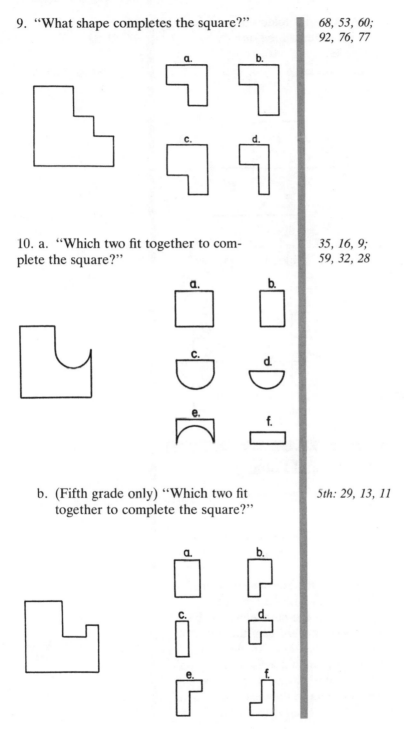

10. a. "Which two fit together to com-   *35, 16, 9;*
plete the square?"   *59, 32, 28*

b. (Fifth grade only) "Which two fit   *5th: 29, 13, 11*
   together to complete the square?"

11. "When this pattern is folded to form a box, which letter will be on the side opposite E?"

20, 6, 7;
73, 63, 32

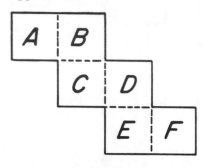

12. (Fifth grade only) "Each pattern can be folded to form a cube. Which two cubes will look the same?"

5th: 49, 26, 44

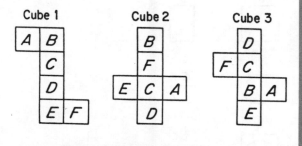

IX. Mental Folding

A. Instructions

1. Record the time it takes the child to finish all the questions. Start to count the time when item 1 is presented.
2. If the child says she/he doesn't know or if 30 seconds have passed without the child answering, go on to the next question. E says, "This is OK. Let's do another one."
3. If the child responds "don't know" to 3 questions in a row, then ask the child if she/he wants to try another one. If the child says "yes," then continue to the next question. If the child says "no," then stop the test.

Practice item: "Look at this picture. Here is 1
and here is 2. Now I am going to fold 1 over 2
like this." The examiner folds 1 over 2. "Now
look down here. Which picture shows what it
looks like?"

If the child points to the incorrect picture, then
repeat the procedure until the child gets the
correct answer. (Only for the practice item.)

If the child points to the correct picture, "That's
right. Now look at this picture. See if you can
tell me the answer. I'll wait for 1/2 a minute."
Present item 1.

B. Problems

1. "Fold B over A. What will it look like?"   *87, 60, 59;*
                                                99, 90, 79

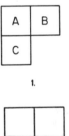

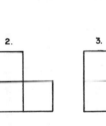

2. "Fold A over B. Fold C over A. What will it   *80, 64, 77;*
   look like?"   *96, 92, 89*

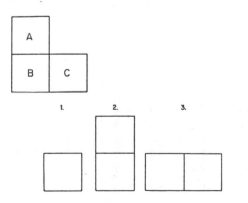

3. "Fold B over C. Fold A over B. What will it look like?"   *88, 68, 72; 96, 98, 98*

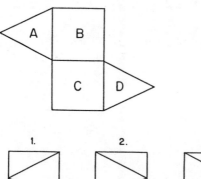

4. "Fold A over B. Fold D over C. What will it look like?"   *73, 60, 51; 94, 80, 82*

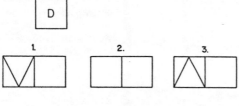

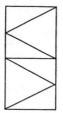

5. "Fold A over B. Fold D over C. What will it look like?"   *71, 42, 41; 95, 82, 80*

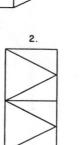

6. "Fold D over B. Fold C over D. Fold A over C. What will it look like?"

78, 46, 44;
93, 88, 82

7. "Fold C over D. Fold B over C. Fold A over B. What will it look like?"

47, 26, 23;
82, 56, 40

8. "Fold B over A. Fold C over A. Fold E over B. Fold D over C. What will it look like?"

52, 25, 15;
86, 68, 48

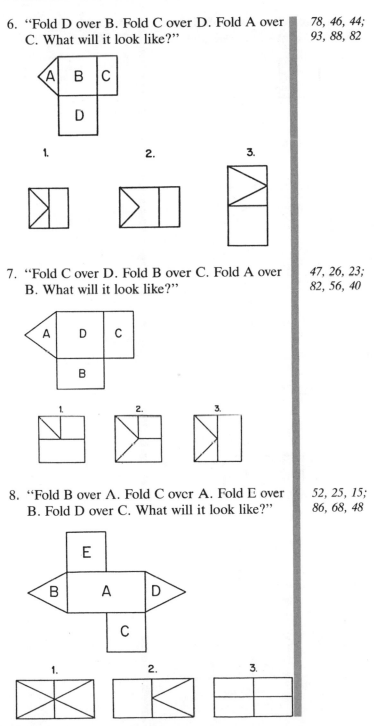

9. "Fold A over B. Fold C over A. Fold D over   *45, 23, 15;*
   E. Fold F over D. What will it look like?"   *87, 71, 66*

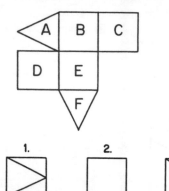

10. "Fold D over C. Fold E over B. Fold G over   *24, 15, 7;*
    D. Fold A over E. Fold F over G. What will   *46, 33, 32*
    it look like?"

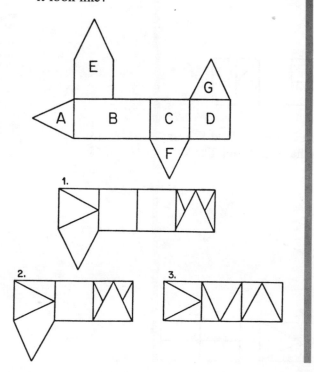

X. Mental Calculation

A. *Instructions*

"Now I am going to show you some problems. I want you to do them as fast as possible. Let's see how many problems you can do in 1 minute. I will point to the problem. You just tell me the answer. You don't have to write the answers down. OK, let's start. I will point to the problem and you tell me the answer."

Time is started when E points to the first problem. E points to the problems from left to right in the horizontal sequence. Record the child's answers on the answer sheet. Stop the child at exactly one minute. Children are not allowed to use paper and pencil for this part of the test.

B. *Problems*

Part A for Grades 1 and 5

A. The following problems are a sample of those shown to the child. A total of 78 problems were presented on three separate pages. All the problems required the addition of two one-digit numbers.

Sample

$$7 + 7 = \quad 5 + 1 = \quad 1 + 4 =$$

$$9 + 7 = \quad 8 + 6 = \quad 6 + 1 =$$

Mean number correct in one minute:

First Grade:
11.0, 8.2, 8.9
Fifth Grade:
37.9, 42.5, 33.2

Parts B–D for Grade 5 only

For parts B and C the examiner uses the same instruction format as in part A.

B. The following problems are a sample of those shown to the child. There were 72 problems in all on 4 separate pages. All the problems were addition of two two-digit numbers.

Sample

$$
\begin{array}{r} 57 \\ +33 \end{array}
\qquad
\begin{array}{r} 69 \\ +84 \end{array}
\qquad
\begin{array}{r} 67 \\ +10 \end{array}
$$

Fifth Grade: 12.2, 14.4, 7.8

$$
\begin{array}{r} 47 \\ +90 \end{array}
\qquad
\begin{array}{r} 76 \\ +99 \end{array}
\qquad
\begin{array}{r} 81 \\ +93 \end{array}
$$

C. The following problems are a sample of those shown to the child. There were 48 problems in all on 3 separate pages. All the problems were multiplication of a double-digit number by a single-digit number.

Sample

$$
\begin{array}{r} 87 \\ \times 32 \end{array}
\qquad
\begin{array}{r} 37 \\ \times 2 \end{array}
\qquad
\begin{array}{r} 38 \\ \times 9 \end{array}
$$

Fifth Grade: 5.8, 7.7, 4.0

$$
\begin{array}{r} 70 \\ \times 3 \end{array}
\qquad
\begin{array}{r} 57 \\ \times 4 \end{array}
\qquad
\begin{array}{r} 51 \\ \times 8 \end{array}
$$

D. "Now I have some difficult problems for you to do. Can you figure out the answers in your head? You can take as much time as you want."

E points to each of the 5 questions and records the time it takes the child to finish each question. Children are not allowed to use paper and pencil for this part of the test.

(Each question appeared on a single page in the test booklet.)

$$
\text{a.}\quad
\begin{array}{r} 15 \\ +26 \end{array}
\qquad
\text{b.}\quad
\begin{array}{r} 415 \\ +376 \end{array}
$$

(a)*90, 96, 82*
(b)*88, 92, 75*
(c)*75, 70, 63*

c.   **28**   d. **409**   e. **28**   (d)*74, 71, 53*

     73   **−156**   **×14**   (e)*44, 44, 9*

  +54